Withdrawn from Stock

Dublin City Public Libraries

784.5 FLE

D0363695

LET ME BEGIN © 2012 Tommy Fleming

Written by Tommy Fleming
Assistant writers Tina Mitchell Fleming & Cathy Fleming
Edited by Alan Morrow
Photograph front cover Marc O'Sullivan
Published by TF Productions Limited
Printed by W&G Baird
Designed by McCadden

ISBN 9780957448308

All photos and text copyright Tommy Fleming & TF Productions Limited.

All rights reserved. No part of this publication may be reproduced, stored in a retrieval system or transmitted, in any form or by any means, electronic, mechanical, photocopying, recording or otherwise, without the written permission of TF Productions Limited.

www.tommyfleming.com

ISBN 978-0-9574483-0-8

9 780957 448308

LET ME BEGIN

By Tommy Fleming

LET ME BEGIN

By Tommy Fleming

Chapter 1
My arrival

Left
The Fleming Family.
I'm age 4 at front.
left-right Belinda, Marie,
Cathy, JJ, with Patrick
in the middle.

I came in to this world on the 15th May 1971. My arrival seems to have been quite calm and quiet, something I can only attribute to the presence of my late father, Paddy. This gentle, softly-spoken man was the most easy-going person I have ever known and I've no doubt his presence would have had a very calming effect on my delivery, and on everyone present at the event. I have often been told that I look like Dad, and while I'm proud of the fact that I bear a physical resemblance to him, I have to say that I certainly didn't inherit his quiet temperament! That part of my character came from my late mother, Annie, a woman who never sat on the fence when it came to speaking her mind. It seems her disarming honesty has been passed on to me through the genes, although it can be a dubious blessing at times.

Dad was a true son of the soil. He was a straight forward, down-to-earth man who loved nature and the outdoors and he held a passionate interest in wildlife and the natural world. It's something all his children have inherited from him. When I was two years old, Dad used to take me along with him when he was out walking over our farm, keeping an eye on our sheep and cattle. I particularly loved springtime, as this was when everything started to come back to life again after winter. I remember Dad patiently explaining what was happening as all the trees and bushes burst into life with new leaves and foliage.

Dad knew where all the fox dens were throughout the farm and he once showed me where a vixen fox was preparing to have her cubs. At the time I didn't understand why he asked me not to tell anyone where the fox dens were, but looking back, I can see he knew I was too young to understand the dangers the foxes faced and this was his way of protecting them. I believe that my protective instinct for all wildlife is one of the greatest traits I have inherited from my Dad, and I'm grateful to him for it. After a couple of hours of these wonderful outdoor adventures, our rumbling bellies would guide us back home. Dad would scoop me up with his huge hands, sit me on his shoulders and carry me home through the fields.

Leabhar   hair Bhaile   ath
blic Libraries

Up there, looking at the world from the safety of Dad's shoulders, I knew nothing could harm me. There have been many difficult times throughout my adult life when I have wished I could return once more to the safety of Dad's shoulders.

I grew up in the townland of Kilmactigue, near the small rural village of Aclare in County Sligo, about 30 miles from Sligo city and 10 miles from Ireland West Airport Knock. Aclare is the nearest village where I spent, or mis-spent, according to my siblings, many happy teenage days.

I was the youngest of six children and definitely the most spoilt, especially by my Mother and my three older sisters. My parents were typical of their generation and they worked hard throughout their lives to provide for us and give us every opportunity they possibly could. We spent our childhood playing outdoors in the fields and hills, trying to capture small animals (which we released again) and using our imagination to turn old bits of wood into cowboy guns. We may not have had all the most fashionable toys of the day, but we had everything we needed and more love than you can imagine.

Above
left-right Belinda, Patrick, Cathy, Me (Age 2), Marie and JJ.

Below
The Fleming Family Home in Kilmactigue.

Chapter 2
My first step into the big world

Left
Fleming Family on summer holidays at Enniscrone beach with cousins Belinda and Dominic Howley.

In 1975, aged just four years old, I started attending our local primary school, Kilmactigue National School, just a couple of miles down the road from our home near Aclare. Looking back almost forty years later, I remember that day as if it were yesterday. I can still see myself holding Mam's hand as she escorted me to my first big day at school, gripping her even tighter when occasional pangs of fear would flood through me. Part of her may have been relieved that her final child was heading off to school. But I suspect she may also have dreaded the fact that the little one who had kept her company every day for four years was now heading off into the big, wide world.

Up until that day, Mam and I had spent a lot of time together while the other five were at school. She treated me as her equal, sharing the news of the day with me and discussing all her thoughts. Those precious hours together laid the foundation for the special bond that we always shared.

That first school day was a typically misty September morning, the sort we had come to expect living half way up a mountain. I can still see the shine on the blackberries and smell the warm, musty air. Every now and then I'd make a break from Mam and run over to investigate any suspicious rustling noises in the briars, hoping to find a rabbit or hedgehog or perhaps an interesting bug. These bursts of freedom were short lived, as Mam would take my hand and hurry me along, scared we might be late for school, as that would have been considered a mortal sin. Mam's grip was always just right – never too tight, but just enough to make me feel safe and secure. I was excited at finally becoming a "big boy" and being able to go to school just like my brothers and sisters. But I was also nervous, with an awful feeling of apprehension in my stomach. I realise now it was a feeling I would experience many times in my life.

We entered the school through two big black iron gates, then came face-to-face with the most enormous door I had ever seen in my young life. I panicked, decided I had changed my mind about school and ran back to the black gates in a bid for freedom! At that moment I'd have given anything to be safe at home or chasing around the farm with my dogs. My short legs carried me as quick as they could, but they were no match for Mam's. She grabbed hold of me, picked me up and carried me through that huge grey door. So, naturally I resorted to a line of defence that I knew always worked on my poor Mam. I bawled my eyes out, pleading and begging to be allowed to go home with her. But nothing worked. I was sat on a chair and she left. I knew then that those magical times when I had Mam to myself were well and truly over.

Below left
My school days.

Below right
Once I learned to write a very important letter to Santa.

Right
School Portrait of The Flemings (Me age 6).

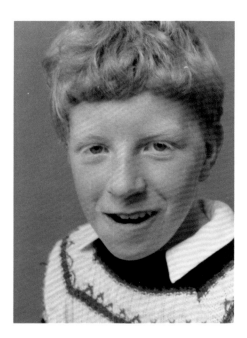

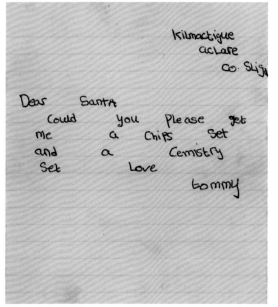

Kilmactigue
aclare
Co. Sligo

Dear Santa
Could you please get me a Chips set and a Cemistry set
Love
tommy

Chapter 3
First celebration

Left
First Holy Communion,
Back row left-right
Fr. Dan O'Mahony, Phil
Touhy, Mary Owens,
Kathleen Doherty.
Middle row left-right
Lorainne Meers, Myra
Rochford, Geraldine
O'Hara, Una Owens,
Geraldine Dunne.
Front row left-right
Jarlath Ginty, Me, Padraig
Walsh, Brendan Quinn,
Pat Price.

For the most part, my primary school years were quite uneventful, with no major highs or lows. My main memory is being sent off every morning with my brothers and sisters and generally going through the motions of school days. However, one happy childhood event is etched into my memory and it remains with me to this day. It revolved around our First Holy Communion. This was a monumental event in my young seven-year old life and our teacher, Mrs Doherty RIP, left no stone unturned when it came to the preparations. She taught us all the prayers and hymns, some of which I have never forgotten and still sing to this day. I'm immensely grateful to her for drilling these songs into our heads and for making sure we could correctly answer any questions that Fr O'Mahony might ask us on the big day.

My favourite part of the build up was when she lined us up to practice receiving the Holy Communion. Now of course, we couldn't receive the real thing, so Mrs. Doherty, in her infinite wisdom, used silvermints in place of the actual host, a much tastier alternative for all us youngsters. My classmate Brendan Quinn and I had the clever idea of messing up our part, so we had to repeat it again and again. After a few too many attempts to get more silvermints, we ended up being made to stand in the corner for punishment. In the end we learned that is what you get for being too greedy.

Mam and Dad also played their part in the preparations for my big day, as a suit, shoes, shirt and fresh haircut were called for. Poor Mam. She spent fruitless weeks trying to find a suit that would fit my small seven-year old frame. Hand-me-downs were out of the question, as they were all too big for me, and with no department stores for miles around, her options were very limited. In the end it was decided that my outfit should be a combination of a new shirt with blue short pants, the smallest blue sandals imaginable and the cutest white socks with a baby whale on each. I can't imagine any seven year old wearing such an outfit today. Anyway, I was now ready for my big day.

To be honest, I only remember some fragments of the day itself, and practically nothing of the ceremony, but I have outstanding memories of the big celebration party afterwards in Auntie Anne's house, with cakes, buns and all the goodies you could eat. I spent most of the day playing in the fields with my brothers JJ and Pat plus all my cousins. We exhausted ourselves outside and returned starved, ready for another fill of the goodies baked in honour of my big day. However, I was met with a frosty reception because of the state I was in.

After a day spent rolling and tumbling in the fields, with no concern for my brand new outfit, the white socks were no longer white, the baby whales had disappeared, the new shirt was torn in several places and a buckle was missing from my little blue sandals. Mam was less than impressed, but she wasn't too hard on me as this was my celebration day, and of course, I was her 'pet'.

Below left
Belinda, Me, Patrick and Cathy.

Chapter 4
My first performance

Left
Performing – where
I'm right at home.

In 1978, I sang in public for the first time. Here's what happened. The end of year school concert was an annual event, put together and performed by all the pupils of Kilmactigue National School. It was held in the local community centre and the all parents, grandparents and relatives of every pupil in the school made sure they were there. It consisted of hours of tuneful (and tuneless) singing, Irish dancing of various standards, haunting dirges played on tin whistles and recorders, and poetry recitals that seemed to last forever.

I performed a song called *Eileen O'Grady* with my classmate Una Owens. We rehearsed endlessly in the weeks leading up to the concert and at times I remember experiencing that strange feeling of apprehension that had gripped me on my first day at school. But the overwhelming adrenalin rush that came with the performance itself is something that will live with me forever. Our prize was a bottle of Cadet red lemonade and a bag of Tayto crisps, we both felt we had done a pretty good job. In fact, for years after the concert I thought our performance had been brilliant, but it was only later that it dawned on me just how terrible it actually was. I clearly remember being driven home that night in our purple Ford Cortina, with Mam and Dad saying how brilliantly we'd performed, and how delighted they were that I'd remembered all the words when so many others stalled, or stood up during a dance and disappeared off stage like lightening.

However, as I write this, an old saying comes to mind: "Every Mother's goose is a swan". So perhaps it's possible that Mam and Dad were just a *little* bit biased about that particular performance.

Chapter 5
Learning more music

In September 1978 I moved into second class with new teacher, Mrs Owens, the mother of Una, my duet partner from the school concert. This meant a new classroom and it was big stuff! I was no longer a small boy any more. Instead, I could look down on all the infants who had just started and the younger children who had only been there a couple of years. Of course, I completely overlooked the fact that I was still physically the same size as the juniors but my self confidence more than made up for that, which meant school life was looking pretty good to me.

At this stage in my education, music, singing and dancing were an important part of the school curriculum. I loved the singing and music. But I wasn't so fond of the dancing, and it got left behind very quickly.

I believe that the encouragement given by Mrs Owens throughout those years helped to carve out the love of singing and music that is now so much a part of my life. We were encouraged to sing and play any instrument we wished and as result, I learned to appreciate and understand many different musical styles and sounds. Looking back on those years, I believe they were the main catalyst in my choice of career.

Chapter 6
New music

By Christmas 1978, aged seven, I was old enough to accompany my brothers and sisters on their annual shopping trip to buy Christmas presents for each other. The best part of this shopping day out was a visit to The Chip Shop to enjoy a plate of chips, washed down by a delicious ice cream soda. The sort of presents we bought for each other were things like bars of soap or 4711 for Mam, bubbles or packets of markers for my sisters and dart guns and such likes for the older lads.

My brother JJ had a part time job, which meant he was the only one of us with any real spending money. The girls and I hatched a cunning plan to try and convince him that the best thing to spend his money on was music. The girls managed to get him to buy the 'Grease' sound track double album and whatever money we had collectively with JJ's was all spent on records. My prize purchase was a forty-five single of Boney M, *By The Rivers Of Babylon*, which featured on the B side of *Brown Girl in the Ring*. That record was played endlessly, until everyone in the house knew every single word of it off by heart. My goal was to be able to perform the song when I returned to school after the holidays. Now that we were beginning to gather our own collection of music we felt that we were discovering something new and wonderful.

Music and singing always played a huge part of our family life. But for me, the new-found freedom of buying a record and playing it, over and over, as loud as possible, was a completely liberating experience, and was in marked contrast to the type of music that featured in our early childhood. We were used to our relatives and neighbours playing traditional music and songs. Now, as we started to buy our own music, we knew there was so much more to discover. Dad was known as an amateur vet or advisor. He was always being consulted about how to treat sick animals or deal with farming problems, there was a constant stream of visitors to our house, which often led to long chats into the night, followed by a tune or the verse of a song.

Chapter 7
Where the music came from

Left
Left-right Fr. Tunny,
Uncle Tony Howley,
Uncle Johnny Boland,
Uncle Brendan Howley.

Probably my earliest memory of music is the Saturday nights we'd spend listening to 'Ceili House' on RTÉ Radio 1. After the compulsory Saturday evening bath for all the children, we would sit around the fire, wrapped in warm towels, with the radio belting out tune after tune, song after song. Uncle Johnny, my dad's Uncle, would listen for any new tunes he could learn to play on the fiddle, and Mam would sing along to all her favourite Irish songs. If the radio wasn't on, then we'd listen to the old red record player in the corner of the living room, spinning scratched LPs of Elvis, Johnny Mathis or Mam's favourite, Jim Reeves.

Our house was always a hive of activity. Relatives and friends would call on a regular basis, and as most of my relatives on both sides were musicians and singers, it never took long for a session to start. I loved those impromptu sessions and I could never stand still, constantly moving from one person to another until at last Dad would scoop me up in those big hands and put me on his lap. There I'd feel safe and happy, watching all the activity from the best vantage point in the room.

My Uncle Johnny Boland senior was a larger-than-life character who had a great influence on me. He was more like a Grandfather to us children, and maybe he deliberately took on this role, as I never knew either of my grandfathers, both of whom died before I was born. Johnny was a man of many talents and a fantastic fiddle player. Every party or celebration that took place in our house, Johnny was there, ever ready with his vast repertoire of tunes and songs. When I was two years old, he took me under his wing and started teaching me to sing. My Dad later told me that Uncle Johnny used to spend hours teaching me songs. One of the songs that still stand out in my memory to this day is *Whiskey on a Sunday*. He even had his own pet name for me, always referring to me as Cushy Buttefield, never as Tommy. Whenever there was a gathering or a party in our house, I'd be asked to sing one of his songs.

I'd take my place on the step between our kitchen and the scullery. To my young mind, that step was my stage and everyone gave me their full attention when I stood there. I made many such performances at home, but the strange thing is that although I can recall all the songs, I don't remember learning them. I think that a combination of listening to everyone singing them, and Johnny's gentle encouragement, stamped them indelibly on my mind.

I also spent many hours in Johnny's house listening to him playing and Johnny gently teaching me new songs. As night closed in and it was getting late, Mam would send one of the other youngsters round to fetch me home, and although I would leave reluctantly, as soon as the opportunity arose the following day I would return. The truth is I never wanted to leave. At birthday parties, Johnny would always insist on entertaining our friends, even though we didn't always appreciate his talent, or so I'm told. He died when I was about five years old, so my only memories I have of him are the songs and tunes he imprinted in my head, and for these I am forever grateful. Fortunately, my Dad kept his memory alive by showing us pictures of Johnny and telling us stories about his life. As a result, I now carry a vivid mental picture of the man and feel as if I know him very well. I've often wondered what he would think if he could see me perform now!

The generations before Johnny also were steeped in music and song. In 1936, my Great-Grandmother, Alice Boland, my Dad's Grandmother, was recorded by the Irish Folklore Commission, singing a Connaught love song that she had been taught by her Grandfather, a hedgeschool master. The recording was made in the Boland home and an article about it appeared in the Irish Press. It recounts that two Grandchildren were present at the recording session, one of whom was my Dad.

My Granny Howley, my Mam's Mother, was a great singer. She would sit in her chair in the middle of the living room, singing songs and telling stories to us children. To us she was like a queen sitting on her throne. Granny Howley was a strong, glamorous woman, I remember

Right
Irish Press, 1936.

Far right
John and Ann Fleming – My Fleming Grandparents.

Below right
Kathleen and Joe Howley – My Howley Grandparents.

THE SHANACHIE TALKS

The Folklore Commission at Work

By L. M.

Domhnall O Cathasaigh, a Kerry Shanachie.

THE wind, sharp with the first snowflakes, whistled round the thatched cottage which had sheltered under the shadow of a huge mountain boulder. From the door it was but a stone's throw to the lake in which a white-mantled peak of the Ox Mountains showed double in the moonlight. The turf fire in the spacious open hearth, burning almost as brightly as the oil lamp on the wall, showed the pleasant, wrinkled features of the grandmother of eighty seated beside the bed in the wall with two little grandchildren nestling near her.

A woman moved about the floor tidying after the evening meal. The other occupants of the kitchen were a couple of grown-up men, a local Irish teacher, two strangers from Dublin, and a straight, gaunt man of nearly seventy, his face furrowed and weather-beaten. He was the local seanchaidhe.

On the table was an instrument that looked strangely out

of place in this remote cottage in the hills of County Sligo, an Ediphone recording machine. An open cardboard box beside it contained a dozen records.

The seanchaidhe told a story in Irish. It was a tale of the rising of '98 with a local setting and interest. After the defeat of the French and their Irish allies at Ballinamuck in County Longford, the redcoats set guards on all the bridges of the Shannon to prevent the Connachtmen's return to their homes. A party of the fugitives constructed a *sgiathóg*. One then swam the river with a rope and the others were pulled across.

Four of the rebels were crossing the mountains to their western homes when they were attacked by seven Protestant men near Kilmacteigue. Each party fired a volley and one of the pursuers fell. They loaded as they ran and a second volley reduced the number of the pursuers to five. A third volley equalised forces. In the circumstances the assailants decided they had had enough and they gave up the chase.

Many years later an old beggarman came from the West and went in to a farmhouse at Kilmacteigue to ask shelter for the night. "Tell us a story," someone suggested as they sat by the turf fire after supper. The beggarman related

his part in the '98 rebellion, the crushing at Ballinamuck, the adventure in this very parish on his way home. "That's no lie for you," said the man of the house quietly, "for I was one of the seven." And he did him no harm, concluded the seanchaidhe.

✧ ✧ ✧

The grandmother sang a sweet Connacht love-song she had learned from her father's father, a poor scholar who settled as a hedge schoolmaster in Gleann an Dá Ghuth, poetically-named Vale of the Two Echoes near Foxford. The seanchaidhe smoked in silence at the fire. A short puff of the clay pipe. An exclamation of approval, "Maith thú!" at the end of each verse. The young children watched the recording machine open-mouthed.

On the hearth a dog was sleeping. A small cat, its fore paws resting on the dog's back, took in the scene with the corner of its eye. Then satisfied there was nothing in it, she rolled herself between the dog's legs and slept.

This is the Irish Folklore Commission at work. Its collectors with Ediphone recording machines are gathering together the folk-tales, songs, local history, ghost stories, fairy tales, traditions, superstitions, everything that portrays or reflects the vanishing life of the

Seán O Clochartaigh, a Galway Shanachie.

countryside. With one of these machines from two to three dozen records, each containing between 1,000 and 1,500 words, can be filled and transcribed in a week. The records are waxcoated; and when the material has been transcribed, the record can be pared and re-used almost indefinitely.

✧ ✧ ✧

Already the archives of the Commission in Dublin contain eighty thousand pages of manuscript materials. By the end of five years the number should have run to five hundred thousand and constitute one of the largest and definitely the most valuable in the world.

Ireland is the only country in western Europe unaffected by the classical Renaissance and the culture of the people has survived here centuries after it has died out elsewhere. She is the custodian of a literary tradition half as old as time, a tradition which is in the possession of those the census calls illiterate. The civilisation of the Middle Ages is here retained in the attic and lumber-room of literature.

We really know very little as yet about the lives of the people of Ireland. How many persons can tell the difference between the haystack of Co. Cork and that of Co. Galway? Or what is the origin of the ordinary Irish farmhouse? Is it Scandinavian, Roman, Bronze Age, or native? Even the language of the Bronze Age is entirely unknown, and the social structure and the laws. We do not even know if Irishmen then lived in houses. Yet probably the Bronze Age man is still alive in Ireland if he can but be put together. The unconsidered trifles of the popular culture are his scattered bones and flesh.

LAND AND WATER.

SWEET VIOLETS

"VIOLET by the mossy stone, half-hidden from the eye" aptly describes the home of a clump of sweet violets now blossoming on a bank under the woods; that conserver of moisture, a mossy stone, right in their centre. A prosperous looking colony, their runners interlace, crossing and re-crossing one with another for a full three feet. A score or more of these sweet smelling flowers —the real wild, white, sweet violet "first-born of the early sun"—were blooming here as is their way, secluded and withdrawn.

In common with many others who are gardeners, I dislike heartily the ant. The only item I know to the credit of this privateer is his habit of distributing the seeds of some plants, including the sweet violet. It is the system called by the very learned a "myrmecochorous" seed distribution and works this way. The seed of the *viola odorata*, or "cool violet," as Spenser calls it, has an oily covering which is so valuable to the ant that for its sake he undertakes the transport of the seed to his nest. On this journey sometimes, tiring of his booty, he will there and then sit down and eat off its oily wrapping, leaving the naked seed to germinate. Or he is perhaps himself attacked by a bird, and the seed being dropped finds new ground on which to start a fresh colony.

The association of the violet with Napoleon is well-known.

K. C. M.

her fondly as being kind and generous to us all. We loved her. One of my favourite Granny Howley songs was an amusing piece called *Tangaloni*. I had no idea what it was about, and I still don't know to this day, but I loved it then and I still remember it very clearly. Another favourite was the *Rocks of Bawn*. She performed it with great enthusiasm and put every bit of effort she had into her delivery, so much so that you believed every word she sang. She could command total silence from her audience, even small children, and she could totally captivate her listeners when she started singing.

My mother was one of ten children, several of whom were outstanding musicians with successful musical careers to this day. Of the six brothers, three were particularly gifted. Pac (Patrick) and Tony followed in their father's footsteps playing the flute, and the youngest, Brendan, played the accordion. Uncle Pac was recorded in the 1950s at the London Irish music sessions playing with Margaret Barry. I can only assume I inherited a bit of talent from both sides of the family.

My Dad's Aunt Kate O'Donnell-Fleming was known for her amazing voice. My Mam would recall how she always sang while working and could be heard from a long way off. When she came to visit us, she never arrived unexpectedly, as we could always hear her singing at top of her voice as she walked up the lane to our house. Mam said I took after Aunt Kate, because like her, I was always singing around the house or while working on the farm. I should add at this point that the sight of me doing any sort of work was a rare occurrence, from what I've been told. I wouldn't say I was lazy. It was more a case of me being completely allergic to hard physical labour. It seems that when it came to saving the hay or turf, I did everything in my power to avoid these tasks. During the summer holidays, the work load on the farm always increased dramatically and everyone had to help out, no matter what! Apparently, I used to disappear during our trips to the bog and while everyone was breaking their backs turning or stacking the turf, I always had an excuse to go walkabout. According to Dad though, I always made it back in time for the grub.

Above left
Mam and Dad's Wedding Day 5th March 1962.

Above right
Uncle Tony on saxophone and John Boland on accordion.

Below
Uncle Johnny Boland, my singing Tutor – looking like a gangster.

Chapter 8
Practice, practice, practice

I may not have had a natural inclination towards hard manual labour, but one job I really did enjoy was milking the cows. When other family members were doing this chore, it normally took about an hour and half to complete. But with me at the udders, it could last anything up to two and half hours.

In my mind, the cow house was a concert hall. You see, I'd discovered that it had amazing acoustics, so while I was milking the cows, I would sing and sing and sing. My parents eventually gave up trying to get me to hurry up with the milking, as it was never going to happen. Once I got in there and started singing I never even noticed that I was working, so I suppose they decided it was better to let me get on with the milking at my own pace, no matter how long it took. God knows what they were thinking as they listened to me singing every song I knew, experimenting with notes and sounds that would shape my future singing style.

I honestly believe this was the best voice training I could have possibly have had, plus it was great practice too. This went on every day, morning and evening, and when the milking was finished and I had finished singing, I removed the milking machines from the unfortunate cows. But there again, who knows – my singing may actually have improved the milk yield!

Chapter 9
New music mixed with the old

As I progressed through primary school and into my final years as a child, I became much more self aware when performing in front of an audience. I think my parents and peers assumed I was just being difficult, but I can see now that it was actually shyness and probably some stage fright. It was around this time that I started to teach myself to play the guitar using a cassette tape and song books. I learned every song I could think of, from *Sloop John B* by the Beach Boys, *Bright Eyes* by Art Garfunkel to the theme song from 'Grizzly Adams'.

The guitar was never out of my hands and I spent hours emersed in playing it. Every time a song I liked came on the radio I would try to copy it as closely as I could. But sometimes, because I didn't have a backing band, I would completely reinvent the sound and do my own alternative version of it. Mind you, it didn't always work! At the time my school Principal, Mrs Phil Touhy, RIP, started to enter me into competitions such as Feis Ceol and Scor Na Og. She insisted that I play traditional ballads but I thought they were unsuitable and found them hard to sing. Instead, I wanted to sing modern hits, not old fashioned tunes, but in hindsight her songs were ideal, so much so that I still sing them and have recorded many of them. It was by following her advice and singing songs such as *Danny Boy*, *Four Green Fields*, *Moorlough Shore* and *Amazing Grace*, that I have been able to follow my present career. I have grown to love these songs and I love performing them. I owe a lot to Mrs Touhy and I am deeply greatful to her for helping to steer me to where I am today.

Chapter 10
Listen, listen, listen

I finished primary school in June 1984 and throughout that summer I listened to all the vinyl records that my family had collected over the years – a collection that was eclectic, to say the least. My Dad was a huge fan of big singers of the '50s and '60s, such as Frank Sinatra, Bing Crosby, Matt Munroe, Barbra Streisand and many more.

I listened to these records for hours on end, digesting every ounce of production on each track, absorbing the way a note was sung, the way a note was held, the way a note was approached. This was the best musical education I could ever have received. Then I discovered that I could hold these notes and keep in tune. From this came my deep conviction that I really wanted to do something in music. I also recognised that I had little or no interest in pursuing other things and that from that point on, it was all about singing and music.

Chapter 11
Now perform

Left
Busking with cousin
Belinda.

During the summer of 1984, Uncle Tony came home from the UK and was due to perform some gigs in local pubs. I was brought along to one of them and this was to be not only my introduction to live gigs, but also my first appearance at one. I was an awkward, self aware thirteen year old, but I was delighted to get the chance to go to the gig in Caulfields pub in Aclare. I was so nervous that when I went on stage to perform, I turned my back on the crowd! My cousin Belinda Howley, the same age as me, was playing the piano. We were both scared and delighted at the same time. To us, this gig meant we were grown up and important enough to be included in the entertainment. We sang *The Isle Of Inisfree* and I have no idea how I remembered the words. Amazingly more than, twenty eight years later, it is still one of the most requested songs at my shows.

After that first live gig, I knew I had a long way to go before I would have the confidence to face an audience at a full concert. I felt I could have performed much better, so I started to experiment with different styles of music and I learned ever more songs. By the time I was about 15, I started performing in pubs, busking on the streets and entering just about every music competition within a fifty mile radius of home. Whether it was a competition for pub talent or street singing, I entered it. Age restrictions meant I was limited in where I could gig, and because I was too young to drive, I always had to persuade someone to take me. Yet somehow I always got there. I remember my long-suffering sister driving me throughout the West of Ireland in her green Toyota K30. It must have been terrible for her, as one of us usually got travel sick in her precious car. Mind you, I'm still not sure whether it was due to our age, or her driving! We christened the car 'Wanderly Wagon' and despite everything, I was grateful for my introduction to the music business.

At each gig I would try out lots of new songs and new musical styles. By now I was getting really quite addicted to the show business bug. I was also gaining in confidence and starting to deliver songs that I knew the audience would like. This was a completely new experience for me. It meant I could now communicate on a different level with people who were listening and reacting to my performances. And it was a million miles away from my private concerts in the cow shed.

Chapter 12
In the money

Left
Me age 19.

One of the benefits of gigging and winning competitions was that I had my first taste of success, and with success, came money... not that much of it ended up in my pockets. Most of the money earned throughout those early years was reinvested in equipment such as mics and speakers and of course, my biggest reward, a brand new guitar. As we started to gain some fame and get a name for ourselves locally, we also started to receive more bookings to sing at wedding ceremonies. To my mind, this was a move in the right direction. Wedding work was high profile, it meant we were performing during the daytime, and, it meant guaranteed fees. There was also the added bonus of more free nights to socialise. As far as I was concerned, this was as good as it could get, and I knew there was nothing else I would be doing for the rest of my life.

Wedding performances were not without their obstacles. It was important to establish what material was suitable for different churches and it was always a battle of wits to keep the brides happy and the priests on side. In general, the grooms couldn't have cared less what we played! So each wedding was a game of politics, juggling between the demands of the church, the priest and the bride. Most priests were easy to deal with, but there were several who flatly refused to allow anything different or modern to be performed in their churches. They would inevitably demand to see a list of the songs we were proposing to sing during the wedding. The result was always the same – a strike of a pen across most of the songs. We quickly learned how to deal with this. There were always two lists! And once we were installed up in the gallery, there was very little anyone could do to change our repertoire.

However, this scheme ran into its own problems when the bookings started to arrive thick and fast and we began to encounter the same priest twice! Sometimes they would come around to the songs after hearing them performed, but there were always the few who refused to change their minds, no matter what. At that point we had to abide by the rules.

TOMMY FLEMING

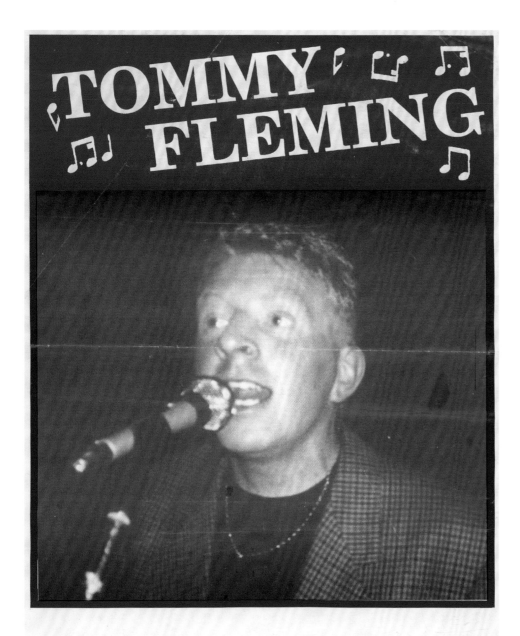

Playing at_____

On_____

Connaught Telegraph, Ellison St., Castlebar

Chapter 13
Planning for the big time

I continued on this musical path throughout my secondary school years until reaching my Leaving Cert year in 1989. Then I decided to form my first band, The Face of Febuary. Most students in Leaving Cert were concentrating on their studies, but not me. I was determined to be lead singer in the biggest band ever, and as far I was concerned I didn't need a Leaving Cert for that. I suppose I was going through my rock phase at this stage, as I was experimenting with tracks from Guns N' Roses, Bon Jovi, Def Leppard and Europe. "Who?" I hear you say. Remember *It's The Final Countdown*?

By now, I was working with electric guitars, keyboards, drums and bass, so I no longer had to improvise with my one acoustic guitar. This meant I could concentrate on the vocals and create the type of sounds I really wanted. Once the band members had been chosen, it was straight into rehearsals. For months these took place in a local community centre and we spent every spare minute there. We meticulously ironed out every chord and note of each song to get them as close as possible to the original sound. After rehearsing to within an inch of our lives, we were ready to unleash the next U2 onto the general public... or so we thought.

I had the great idea of staging our first concert in the school gym hall, so I approached the school principal, Paddy Tobin, and got a definite "NO!". Despite this set back, I took on the role of promoter and manager and I booked our show into Kilmactigue Community Centre, the very same place in which I had made my first stage appearance at the age of seven. The date for the show was 27th December 1989. We designed our own posters and started to promote our very first concert. No telegraph pole, shop window or notice board was safe. We plastered posters everywhere and the buzz started to take off...

December 27th arrived and a palpable sense of anticipation rippled through us all. Or perhaps it was blind fear. The dread of what lay ahead was terrifying. We had a million questions about the performance. How would it sound? Would anyone bother to turn up? Our carefully chosen outfits consisted of ripped jeans with Doc Martin boots and plastic biker jackets (we couldn't afford leather ones) and our aim was to look as cool as possible. We sound checked and double sound checked, by showtime, we were wrecked.

The concert kicked off at 10.00pm and to our surprise there were around 200 people in the audience, although only about fifty had paid to get in. The guest list was huge because each of us had asked all our family and friends to attend, for fear no one else would turn up. We had also invited a bunch of so-called friends, all of whom claimed they were best mates with one of us to avoid the £2.50 cover charge. But to be honest, we didn't really worry too much about all that. Once the place was packed, we sang and played our hearts out with a full two hour set list that ranged from *Sweet Child O' Mine* by Guns N' Roses, to *Money For Nothing* by Dire Straits. The concert was rocking and the experience was amazing. But although I thoroughly enjoyed the night, I knew that something just wasn't right. I had to figure it out!

I quickly found the answer. This music was not for me. I had got the rocker out of my system and that was it. That was the one and only show I ever did with the Face Of Febuary. On reflection, it was probably a selfish and immature decision, considering how hard the rest of the band had worked on the project. We had put in many hours of hard graft and now that was that, it was over. Time for me to move on. The band continued for a number of years after my departure.

Mam was never happy about the rock band thing, and as far as I can recall, this was the only time she ever disapproved of something I was working on. The fact that the rest of the band were in their twenties and early thirties probably didn't help matters either. I suspect she

Below left
Poster for the Face of
Febuary concert.

Below right
With cousin Seamus
O'Donnell at Lough Talt
1991.

knew it wasn't a good idea for an eighteen year old to be hanging out with much older mates and yes, I learned stuff I probably shouldn't have during that time. In hindsight, I was far too young and immature to be involved in this type of band. However, I still have a secret smile to myself when I hear some of those songs, and what's even funnier is that I still remember most of the lyrics to songs like *Sweet Home Alabama* and *Born In The USA*. And yes, I still perform them from time to time during a good karaoke night on holiday or at a party.

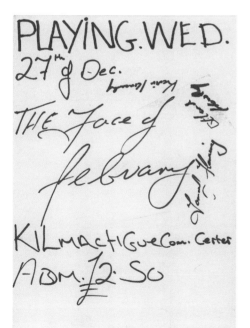

Chapter 14
Education? So what!

Upper left
Me with Ciaran Loftus.

Upper right
On Croagh Patrick.

Below
House party with
Left-right Kieran
O'Donnell, Seamus
O'Donnell on whistles,
Marie, Me, and Maureen
O'Hara holding words
of the song.

January 1990. A new year, a new decade. I had only six months left until the end of term and I honestly didn't care about school. All I cared about was wishing the time away so that I could finish school. Mam and Dad never pressured me to work hard but they made sure I stayed at school to complete my final exams. I suppose they hoped I just might see the importance of education before it was to late. But to my mind, school was holding me back from what I wanted to do most of all – pursue my music career. The last six months at school passed quickly, and before I knew it, final exams, The Leaving Cert, were upon me. I didn't bother too much with revision work or any kind of exam preparation. I simply went in to the examination room, answered the papers as best I could and just about scraped through. I have very few regrets in my life, but I truly wish I had worked harder during my education and made more of the opportunity at the time. That said, even if I had studied harder, I don't believe it would have made any difference to my choice of career.

By the summer of 1990, I was free. I was nineteen and I had the use of Dad's car, so I could gig more or less anywhere I wanted and I didn't need anyone to escort me. I was booked for shows almost five nights a week, I was earning a good living and I was having a great time, learning more and more each time I performed. However, something still wasn't right. There was something still missing. I wanted more from music, and pub gigs were not the answer. I entered more and more pub talent competitions, winning some, losing others, but I never stopped striving to improve my talent and searching for that elusive answer to what was missing.

Chapter 15
My chance at fame

Left
An early performance.

Throughout the summer and autumn of 1990, our local radio station, Mid West Radio, ran a talent competition called The Zanussi Entertainer of the Year. Entrants had to send in a demo tape and the lucky contestants would be selected from these and given a chance to perform live in the heats. I had no recordings of my singing so I had to improvise. I got out my tape recorder and checked every room in the house for its sound qualities and acoustics. None of the rooms were suitable, so I resorted to my old reliable, The Cow House! Once again my concert hall came to the rescue. Its acoustics were amazing (and still are).

I submitted my version of an old Irish ballad, *Skibbereen*, performing it numerous times until I got a demo that I was really pleased with. When my tape was completed, Mam rushed it to the local post office to make sure it was sent off in safe hands. Dad must have thought I had lost my mind, watching me sing my head off in The Cow House where I'd spent so much of my youth. There I was again, an adult, but still doing exactly the same thing. I'm sure it crossed his mind and our neighbours who could hear me that I was completely mad but he never passed any comments. He just glanced in when he was passing and gave me a gentle smile. I knew it was his way of telling me he approved, even though not a word passed his lips.

The week after Mam sent my tape to Mid West Radio, I received a phone call telling me I had been chosen to sing live on air in one of the heats. Now all I had to do was perform well enough to win my heat and qualify for the grand final. The first prize was £1,000, which was a very substantial amount of money back then. In addition, there was the bonus of airplay on your local radio station, plus a live broadcast every Sunday night from the competition but I'd only get all this if I was successful in the heats. This was it. I had the recording bug and the challenge of getting my recording played on the airways. I was off... or so I thought!

Two weeks later I drove with Mam, Dad, my sister Belinda to Ballyhaunis in County Mayo, to a nightclub called 'Midas'. I was one of five competitors due to perform, and only two of us would be chosen to go through to the next round. I was listed to appear fourth out of the five and the song I had chosen to sing was Brendan Behan's classic *The Auld Triangle*. It would be an accapella delivery, with no musicians or band to support me. I was totally alone and when I took to the stage to sing my song, I delivered every word with gusto. The night passed slowly as the radio station dragged out every minute to fill the allotted time and hold onto its listeners at home. But that was of little consolation to those of us waiting patiently for the results. I honestly didn't think I would get through, so I just wanted to get out of there as quickly as possible.

Finally, we got to the results. After a long drawn out process, the first successful entry was called out. Then there was another delay! I felt was about to boil over but my parents looked as cool and calm as ever. I started to get mad at them – how the hell could they remain so cool when I was falling apart! Just as I was about to explode, my name was called out. I was through! WOW. What a shock!!

Three weeks later the second heat was upon me. I had rehearsed at length and I was determined to give an even better performance this time. I really wanted to qualify for the final and win the big prize money and airplay. My Mam and Dad and my three sisters, Marie, Cathy and Belinda, came along to support me. They were more nervous and anxious than me because they'd all realised that this was now a serious competition! The excitement didn't end there. The Sunday night radio broadcasts had caught the attention of every man, woman and child in the West of Ireland and it had become a programme not to be missed. This was long before X Factor, or any similar programmes, but it was designed along the same lines and its aim was to get everyone emotionally involved.

My preparations went on all day. I choose my outfit and then Mam carefully ironed it. The girls were excited too, as this was a big night out for them. Huge crowds would be there and the craic would be mighty. And of course Dad had to make sure all the jobs on the farm were completed, so we could get away on time, dressed to kill! I tried to be as laid back as possible, which is in complete contrast to my personality, as any member of my family will happily testify. Then off we set to Ballyhaunis, a distance of only twenty miles but that night it felt like two hundred.

Once again I was one of five contestants, but this time I was told I would be up first! This news completely freaked me out. I hated the thought of being first because it meant I'd have no idea what the other competitors were like. Not only that, I'd then have to sit through the whole night waiting and wondering. Well, so be it. I focused instead on my song, a more contemporary number called *Bright Blue Rose* by Jimmy McCarthy.

A backing band was provided for this performance but I had no chance to sound check or rehearse with them. To be honest, I found them more of a hindrance than a help. The band decided the song should be played country and western style and I desperately tried to get them to understand that I wanted the song to be played as a much folkier sound. But my suggestions fell on deaf ears. The more I pushed, the further they drifted! I sang the song as well as I possibly could, but I thought I sounded like a cross between Garth Brooks and Willie Nelson. When I finished this horrendous version of an amazing song, I took a hurried bow, acknowledged my applause and left the stage as fast as I could. I was gutted, convinced I had completely messed up my chances.

That night there was a larger than usual audience as the competition momentum was building and everyone wanted to be there. This added to the atmosphere and excitement of the night, but put me further into a spin and tied me up in knots. After my performance I went back to my family and everyone tried to convince me that I'd sounded great and not to worry. But I was disgusted. My Mam said it was brillant. Dad just said not to worry, as he knew that my version of *Bright Blue Rose* was a million miles from any country and western version. None of what they said mattered because I still thought that in my attempt to introduce an original new song had backfired on me. I also knew that I had no desire to become a country and western singer.

The rest of the night passed quickly. I suppose I'd made up my mind that it had all gone wrong and there was no way I could possibly qualify for the final. At last the time came to announce the finalists. The first act to get through to was a singer called Unan McCormick from Tubbercurry in County Sligo. I was resigned to the fact that I wasn't going through. Then the second act was announced and to my shock and absolute disbelief, it was me. I was stunned!

Left
Rob Thornburgh on fiddle
and Michael Buckton on
guitar at a local gig.

Chapter 16
It's the final countdown

The final for the Zanussi Entertainer of the Year competition was due to take place in December 1990. The date had been set but snow and icy conditions caused the event to be postponed until January 1991. Given my experience with the backing band in the second heat, I was apprehensive about trying to rehearse too much before the competition, but in the end I decided to do some preparation, just in case.

I also decided I was not going to get caught out by an unknown backing group, so this time I arranged to bring my own musicians to accompany me on the night. My new band consisted of my first cousin, Belinda Howley, on keyboards, Colm O'Donnell, my second cousin on accordian and whistle, and Michael Collins, my former science teacher, on guitar. They were all used to my style of singing. Our preparations together meant that this time around, I was in a much more relaxed frame of mind.

For the competition final, each contestant had to perform two songs. I chose *The Auld Triangle* and an old Scottish folk song called *Anachie Gordon*. My thinking on this choice was that since the Scottish song had around eight verses, it would give the judges more time to hear me. Of course, it never entered my head that I might just bore them to death.

On the big night, the venue was packed to capacity. My entire family were there, including a support team of friends and relatives from home. When we arrived, all ten finalists had to meet back stage and we were given full instuctions about what was going to happen during the night. We were told the running order, where we had to be and when. I was going to be second last to perform and I felt that with all my experience behind me, I was very well prepared. That said, I was still very nervous but nowhere near as nervous as my band members. At last my name was called, and the three musicians and I walked on stage together. I can still see Michael Collins' face – he looked so nervous I thought he was going to pass out. None the less, we went on, took our positions, and performed our set.

I sang my two songs to the best of my ability, took my bow and left the stage. The musicians had been brillant. Each of them had held their nerve and delivered a flawless performance. What's more, I had enjoyed every note of the performance because I'd been able to sing the songs the way we had rehearsed them. The atmosphere in the nightclub was electric, with an intoxicating mix of excitment and anxiety as we waited for the results to be called. The place was full of supporters for all the contestant and each group had their favourite. Finally, after a couple of hours, the results were about to be announced. Three places were to be awarded. I would have happily settled for any one of those places. We all waited in silent anticipation, with the tension rising to an unbearable level.

First to be announced was the the third place act. This was followed by the second place and still no mention of me. Just when I thought all was lost I heard the compere say "...and in first place, Tommy Fleming!". I couldn't believe what had just happened. My supporters went wild. My two brothers picked me up and carried me on their shoulders around the room in a victory procession, with my Dad proceeding alongside, holding my hand. It was the first time I had ever seen my Dad cry. He was bursting with pride, not just for me, but for all of us. Nothing could compare to the happiness he felt that night. His overwhelming emotion made us equally emotional. I will never forget that feeling and I'm sure I'll never fully appreciate the effect it had on Dad. My Mam was a little more reserved in her joy and she waited for all the madness to calm down before she came over to give me a hug and a kiss. It was as if she knew the result in advance and wouldn't have expected it to be any other way. Eventually I pulled myself together, sang my songs again and was given my cheque for £1,000 punts.

I was the happiest man on earth that night.

Chapter 17
Jarrog is born

Once the initial exitement of my win had calmed down, I spent the the following weeks planning and plotting ways to further my musical career. As always, I reinvested my winnings into better equipment. I bought a new PA system and started approaching some of the bigger pubs and clubs for bookings. With the creditability of my win under my belt, it was easier to secure bigger venues and bigger fees.

I decided to form another band with one of my cousins, Seamus O'Donnell, who played flute and whistles. Also to join us was Martin Bolger on guitar and Rob Thornburgh on fiddle, mandolin and hammered dulcimer, an instrument that sounds remarkably like a piano. I'd never played with one of these before and it was a welcome new sound to experiment with. The band was christened Jarrog, pronounced Dearg, which is Gaelic for red and was an obvious reference to my flame-coloured locks.

J'ARROG

'As the Light Declines'

PLAYING IN
TEACH MURRAY
GURTEEN
SAT. MAR 7th.

Chapter 18
NO!

Above left
Cathy and Me at my
21st Birthday.

Above right
1992 Poster from
Mitchelstown Festival.

Below left
Jarrog Poster.

Below right
Left-right Seamus
O'Donnell, Me, Rob
Thornburgh, Jarlath
McTiernan, Frankie
McFadden – Jarrog.

During these early years my sister Cathy and I set about trying to secure a record deal. We knocked on the doors of every record company in Dublin, but the answer was always the same. NO. We approached numerous record companies, but the only one that showed any interest at all was Harmac Records, a small independent label that was home to artists such as Paddy Reilly, the Clancy Brothers and other well known folk artists of the time. We had several meetings with Harmac, and things were looking positive. We thought we were heading in the right direction, but nothing materialised and no offer came our way, so we went back to knocking on doors again.

I found this constant rejection by the record companies to be thoroughly demoralising, so I decided the only answer was to record an album by myself. I set about gathering songs for the album and soon I had recorded Jarrog's first album, *As The Light Declines*. I do believe that for a first attempt it was really quite good. However, in retrospect, the cover is very embarrassing and I really hope that, as with all the best things in life, it will improve with age! We sold cassette tapes of our new release at gigs and in every local shop that would take them... sometimes even from the boot of our car!

I sent a copy of *As The Light Declines* to every radio station in the country in the hope of getting some airplay, but with little success. I can't be sure but I honestly think it probably only received air play on our local radio staion, and that was mainly due to Mam's incessant phone calls requesting they play it. We performed up and down the country, in every type of venue you could think of, and before long we had secured a residency in two of the best music venues in Sligo – TD's and The Leitrim Bar. This meant that on Tuesday, Thursday and Sunday of every week, we were guaranteed a gig. It was a massive boost to our morale and was followed by a steady flow of gigs that kept coming our way. These gigs continued over the next couple of years, with different musicians joining from time to time to expand and improve the sound. By the end of 1992 we were appearing all over the country and even getting bookings for summer festivals. We loved these, as they paid good fees and provided accommodation, which meant we could stay and enjoy the craic. Two of the highlights during our visits to these festivals were the Mitchellstown Deer Festival and the Feakle Irish Music Festival, where we shared the bill with Steve Cooney and Seamus Begley. I saw this as a huge achievement. Things seemed to be moving in the right direction and I felt I was getting closer to performing at concerts, where people came purely to enjoy the music. I knew now that this had been my ultimate goal from the start. I just hadn't realised it until that moment.

Below left
My entry for RTÉ Live at 3 'Search for a Star'.

Below centre
My first TV Appearance, RTÉ's 'Big Top' in 1993.

Below right
Left-right Alan Kelly on accordion, Me, Martin Bolger on guitar and Rob Thornburgh on fiddle.

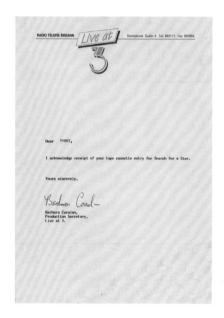

Chapter 19
The break!

By the start of 1993 we were still performing all over the country and taking bookings for any type of gig we could get. Music was now my full time job and I was loving every minute of it. But I knew that things were still not quite right and that I needed to progress to the next stage. I just didn't know how to get there.

After making numerous calls and knocking on countless doors throughout that summer, we finally struck gold with our first TV appearance on a show called The Big Top, with presenter BB Baskin. The show was recorded in a circus tent in Castlebar and was due to be broadcast later that summer. I sang a song called *The Grip Of Parallel* by Jimmy McCarthy. It was like winning the talent contest all over again. The buzz of a high profile television appearance was intoxicating and suddenly I started to get attention from outside my local area. I landed a few other high profile support slots and one of the biggest was opening for the Womens Heart concert in the National Stadium in Dublin. There was an audience of around 2,000 people that night, one of the biggest crowds I had ever performed to, it was scary but exhilarating. I got a fantastic reaction from the crowd and that heightened my desire to achieve bigger and better things.

A few weeks later I secured another TV appearance on a special show commissioned to celebrate Mayo's 5,000 years. The show was recorded in the National Concert Hall in Dublin and once again I performed *The Grip Of Parallel*. I shared the bill with a number of acts, including at that time an unknown American dancer called Michael Flatley. The show was also scheduled to be broadcast later in the year. This gave my career a much needed boost. At last I felt that I was performing in the right venues, singing the type of music I wanted to perform. Having had a taste of this, I didn't want to go back.

In July of 1993 I performed at a charity event in a marquee in Westport, County Mayo. I had just finished my first set and was taking a break when I was introduced to Phil Coulter, who was a guest at the function. By this time Phil had already established his hugely successful career as a songwriter, performer and producer and he was a highly influential figure in the Irish music industry. We chatted for a while about my musical influences and where I wanted my career to go. He was curious as to what type of music I would like to record, although our opinions differed as to what direction my career should take musically. After our initial chat, I returned to the stage and invited Phil to join me for a song. He kindly obliged and we performed *The Leaving Of Liverpool* together, for which we received a standing ovation! This was it. This is what it's all about! We chatted at length after the show and he asked me to call him in his office later that week.

I called Phil as promised and during our discussion he invited me to join him and his orchestra on their Irish tour as a guest vocalist. This was exactly the break I had long been looking for, and I knew this was the precise direction I wanted to go in. We had several meetings and telephone conversations regarding the style of music I would perform throughout his Irish tour and once this was all agreed, arrangements were made for me to start attending rehearsals immediately.

I arrived at the Factory rehearsal studios near the old Boland biscuit factory in Ringsend, Dublin. I was extremely nervous and more than a little apprehensive about how all of this was going to pan out. It was the first time in my career that I had ever been directed by someone else. Phil's band were set up and ready to go. I had to wait for an hour or so and then Phil sent his tour manager, Roy Dixon, to bring me into the studio for the rehearsal. I'm not ashamed to say that I was terrified of what lay ahead.

I walked into a huge room, covered in black drapes and mirrors. I took one look around and spotted flight cases everywhere. This was it! Proper rehearsals. It all looked very rock and roll. I felt I was home and knew that this was what I had been dreaming of for years. It was certainly quite a change from the cold cow shed or singing in a community centre with no proper sound equipment. All of that had been an important part of my learning process,

Below left
David Hayes and myself
ready to go on stage.

Below right
David in recording studio.

but now it was wonderful to find myself in a real rehersal studio, with proper equipment… somewhere I could deliver my songs and know they would be heard the way I wanted them to be heard. I took my place at the mic and sang the first of three songs, *The Leaving Of Liverpool*, followed by *Loving Hannah* and finally, my trusted favourite, *The Auld Triangle*. All went well and I loved every second of it. I couldn't wait to start performing live in front of an audience.

After rehearsals I collected my music sheets and the time came to get the full introductions. Phil introduced me to the band and I met David Hayes for the first time. He continued to work with me, and twenty years later, we remain partners. He is my musical director on all my tours and new releases. Our relationship has developed and deepened over the past twenty years, following that first meeting at rehearsals in the Factory in 1993.

Chapter 20
The Big Stage

Left
Phil Coulter and me on
stage on the first Irish
tour, 1993.

By June of 1993 the time had come for the first of several shows with Phil Coulter and his orchestra. Our opening concert was in the Cork Opera House. After the sound check I couldn't wait to get going. Everything was ready and as I waited back stage to be called for my set, I felt quite confident, as I knew this was exactly what I was supposed to be doing and I had long dreamed of having my own concert in this type of venue. That night I only had to perform three songs, but my ambition was to do a full show of my own.

When my time arrived, I walked on stage and launched into my first performance. Then disaster struck. My mind went completely blank and I realised I had forgotten the lyrics of *The Leaving Of Liverpool*. What seemed like an unmitigated disaster was quickly rescued by the other musicians. They manoeuvred their way around the song and gave me time to recover and continue with my performance. This was the first of many important lessons in professionalism. Never, ever underestimate your performance or forget where you are performing! EVER.

We played to almost 3,000 people over the three nights in Cork Opera House, then it was off to Dublin for a series of concerts in the National Concert Hall. To be honest, after the three Cork concerts, I felt like an old pro. This was another mistake which reflected my complete naivity at that time. One thing I have learned about the music industry is that after twenty years in it, I still have much to learn.

Dublin was a very special show and it remains a huge milestone in my career. To this day, many of the amazing people I meet at my shows tell me that the first time they heard me sing was in the National Concert Hall with Phil in 1993. Throughout that summer, I performed in eight shows with Phil and the orchestra but I also continued to keep my club and pub gigs going.

Towards the end of summer I was asked if I would accompany Phil and the band for a six-week tour of North America and Canada. I don't know which was more exciting – the prospect of seeing the USA and Canada for the first time, or the fact that my singing would be heard by an estimated audience of over 100,000. My excitement reached its peak when I discovered I would perform in New York's legendary Carnegie Hall on the 1st December, 1993. I couldn't believe what was about to happen and I knew this was going to be the biggest night of my life! Around this time I also started to receive a lot of attention from local press and radio. My 1991 recording was getting a lot of airplay on local radios and two of the songs in particular were being constantly played – *The Isle Of Inisfree* and *Loving Hannah*. Both of these tracks would feature as part of Phil Coulter's USA tour.

Below left
Gay Byrne, Presenter, The Late Late show with Cathy and Me.

Below right
Chatting to Gay Byrne after the show.

Chapter 21
My silent TV performance

In October 1993, I got a phone call from a lady called Bridget Ruane, a researcher on RTÉ's The Late Late Show. This was and still is the biggest chat show on Irish television. It has been on air for fifty years and is still going strong. Bridget had heard my recording of the *Isle Of Inisfree* on the radio and wondered if I would be interested in performing it live on The Late Late Show. The answer was a resounding YES! So, in mid-October, I went to RTÉ in Dublin to perform live on the biggest TV show in Ireland. I remember spending days wondering what it would be like to perform live and worrying about all the things that could go wrong. I'm sure I changed my mind about forty times about what to wear. Eventually I chose a black shirt, multi coloured waistcoat and bottle green trousers. Trendy then, hideous now!

I arrived in RTÉ with my sister Cathy, who was my support for the night. We were greeted and introduced to the show's producers, researchers and directors. Then it was straight to work and I was escorted into the studio where I got a chance to rehearse my song, accompanied by three backing musicians. The afternoon was full of camera checks, sound checks ,camera angles, lighting and more sound checks. Finally, I was ready for my appearance, live on TV. I was given my schedule time for makeup, wardrobe told where to go and where to be. As the time for the show approached, my nerves really started to kick in.

The show went on air at 9.30pm and had an estimated audience of three quarters a million people. Its format comprised a mix of chat, comedy and music. I was scheduled to appear at the start of the second half of the show, which ran for a total of two hours, so I had some time to wait, which is never good when you are nervous. Eventually the stage manager came for me and escorted me to wait in the wings, which I did very obediently. I was then brought out into the performance area and waited patiently to perform. While I was standing there I watched the host, Gay Byrne, conducting an interview with Roger Moore, the former James Bond. All I knew was that I had no feeling in my legs. I was consumed with nerves and couldn't wait to get it over with!

When the interview concluded, Gay moved to the next item of music, which was me. His introduction seemed to go on forever, while I was nearly passing out with nervous exhaustion. Just as I was about to turn tail and run, the music started and Frank McNamara played the intro to *The Isle Of Inisfree*. After about fifteen seconds of an intro, it was my cue to start singing. I opened my mouth for the first lines of the song, only to discover the battery in my mic was dead. It was the one of the few times my inexperience actually helped me. If I had been more experienced with TV, I may well have lost my head at such a monumental cock up, but as it was, I just continued singing with no mic! What I didn't realise was that an over head mic was able to pick up my voice and the sound carried. I just put my head down and concentrated on my performance and delivered as best I could with no mic.

When my song was over the audience reaction was amazing, as were Gay Byrne's parting words. I still can hear them today. "That was outsanding" he said. He also referred to the audience in Carnegie Hall, New York, saying "there wouldn't be a dry eye in the house". I was ecstatic. I felt like I had just won the lotto. I left the floor and headed back to the green room for a drink and a post mortem on my performance.

My first instinct was to ring home. In 1993 it was a big deal to appear on The Late Late Show and it still is. Despite their usual calm selves, I could hear the emotion and pride in my parents' voices.

I was told afterwards that my parents had waited patiently all day for the show to begin and that they had watched it intently at home. Of course Mam couldn't wait to get to mass the next day as she knew everyone would be commenting on it and she could pretend she didn't enjoy all the attention.

Chapter 22
Up and away

By late October 1993, I was all set for my trip to the United States of America. In the days before I left, my poor broken-hearted Mother helped me pack and repack my new suitcase. She was both delighted and upset at the thought of my trip – delighted that I was getting this big chance, but scared stiff that I might like it too much! She said very little during our packing and organising. Dad said nothing, as he probably sensed it would only send my Mam into another bout of crying and praying. Inwardly though, he was delighted for me, as he knew that this was exactly what I needed to move my career forward. When it came time to leave, I said my goodbyes and got the usual soaking of holy water and blessings. And of course a candle was lit that wouldn't be extinguished until my return.

I headed off for Dublin airport where I met with the rest of the band and crew. The tour manager got us all organised, and after several hours dealing with security, immigration and filling our stomachs, we eventually boarded the flight for New York City. Seven hours later, we touched down in JFK International airport. We were due to catch a connecting flight but I wanted to take a quick look around JFK airport to get an idea of what New York might be like. I was so excited and giddy! I felt like a child on a school tour. I couldn't wait to see the city that had captured my imagination for years and now, I was here! This was magic.

After I disembarked the plane, the culture shock of stepping into the airport hit me like a runaway train. I had never experienced so many diverse cultures all together under one roof. I couldn't believe how loud everything and everyone was. The volume of this crazy place was a million miles from my home and was unlike anything I had experienced in all my 22 years. I realised I was behaving like a bog-trotting tourist, but I couldn't stop looking all around me, completely amazed at everything I saw. My senses were being assaulted on every level, from the overwhelming smell of cinnamon, to the different languages I could hear all around me. There were so many different nationalities all bustling and vying for a space in this magical world of JFK airport.

We eventually boarded our connecting flight to Denver, Colorado for the opening night of the tour. This was to be followed by visits to cities all over the USA and Canada for the next six weeks. We arrived in Denver International Airport, cleared customs, collected our bags and made our way to the hotel. By now we were totally exhausted and all anyone could think about was getting to bed. The initial excitement I'd felt on arrival in New York had long since gone. I decided to hit the sack and resume the tourist trail tomorrow.

Left
left-right James Paul Murphy, Austin Walsh, Trish Buckley, Me, Grainne Kelly in New York.

Chapter 23
The Reaction!

We spent the next three days in Denver which was great because my sister Belinda was living there. I was able to spent a couple of days with her before the opening night. Denver was my first USA show, I was so full of energy and attitude, ready to take on the world.

The opening night was sold out, so I was already nervous, but the fact that my sister was in the audience added to my sense of panic. I wanted my performance to go well! Then my turn came and I took to the stage for my first two songs. All went according to plan, I remembered the words and the mics worked fine. I finished to a thunderous applause, took my bow and exited stage right. I realised that the audience must have liked it and this gave me the confidence to deliver an even better performance in the second half.

When I came back on stage to sing my final two songs, closing with *The Auld Triangle*, I was completely stunned when I got a standing ovation from the packed house in Denver. I was on top of the world and this lifestyle suited me very well indeed!

Chapter 24
My introduction to culinary delights

The after show party was held downtown in a traditional Irish pub, which featured a very untraditional finger buffet, including rattlesnake and other delicacies. Being a young, growing Irish lad, I was always hungry, but the only food that looked in any way familiar was a dish called Rocky Mountain Oysters. It resembled chicken nuggets, so I tucked in and had a good feed of them. Imagine my reaction when I found out that Rocky Mountain Oysters were in fact bulls testicles, sliced, breaded and deep fried! That was my introduction to the many different culinary delights I have sampled and enjoyed during my years of travel. But believe me, after that experience, I quickly learned to politely ask first, before eating.

When all the excitement and hype of our opening night had calmed down, our next port of call was the amazing city of San Francisco. By now I had completely settled into the American way of life and was loving every minute of it. The tour played to packed houses across the USA and Canada, but it wasn't all plain sailing. By the time we reached New York, about five weeks into the tour, I was ready to go home. I loved the USA and all it had to offer but we were travelling everywhere by bus, and despite the fact that it was utterly luxurious, with TVs, fridges, separate sleeping areas and everything we might need, we were confined in this small space for hours on end, and everyone was now getting on each other's nerves. It was time to dig deep and shut up, so as to avoid any unnecessary blowups. But being 22 and a red head, this wasn't always possible!

Just as things were about to explode, we arrived in New York en route from Boston and made our way to Manhattan via Harlem. This was the biggest eye opener I had ever experienced. The only part of New York I had seen prior to then was JFK airport. I couldn't believe what I was seeing... the lights... so many people... the high rise buildings... it was awesome. We checked into Fitzpatrick's Hotel in Manhattan and once we were off the tour bus, the tension disappeared and the excitement of being in New York replaced any longing to go home.

With three days off before the show, I took in all the sights of New York. I met up with old school friends who had emigrated to the USA and were now living in this wonderful city. I soaked up all it had to offer and after three days, I felt like a native New Yorker. I was loving it.

Performance day finally arrived on 1st December 1993. I would be singing in Carnegie Hall, one of the most prestigious music theatres in the world. I was like a little child on Christmas morning who hadn't slept the previous night. Rehearsals were scheduled for 3.00pm on the afternoon of show day. I walked all the way down Fifth and Sixth Avenues, eventually making my way to 881 Seventh Avenue on 57th Street to arrive at Carnegie Hall. I rang the call bell at the stage door several times before someone finally answered and after a barrage of security questions due my lack of identification, I was finally allowed enter the great building itself. I was led down the corridor to my dressing room and then onto the stage for rehearsals and sound checks. At that point I was then informed that there was a slight change to the programme for this show. Phil had included *Silent Night* to my list of songs! "No problem", I thought to myself. However, there was a catch. It had to be sung in Irish... As Gaeilge.

Actually, the prospect of singing it in Irish wasn't too daunting, as I had sung it in my native tongue as a child. I just needed to re-boot my memory! The show started on time at 8.00pm sharp and soon it was my turn to grace the stage of this historic building. My stage fright was almost overwhelming, so much so that I was sick for the very first time in my life. I was in such a state of panic I couldn't get a grip on anything, but on I went, sang my heart out and received the first standing ovation of the night. I exited the stage, taking a bow of appreciation for the wonderful audience and for a brief moment, the nerves were gone. But I still had to perform *Silent Night*. Fortunately my nerve held as I took to stage for my second performance of the night. I breezed through it until the very last line, which I completely forgot! It was time to improvise, so I simply repeated the previous line. Another experience, another new lesson. And I still had a lot more to learn!

The show concluded with Phil taking several bows and performing three encores. I was brought back on stage to take my final bow. I felt on top of the world and I still couldn't believe I had performed in this iconic building. After the concert there was a 'meet and greet' party hosted by the promoters in one the Hall's main reception rooms. It was mainly for close friends and family and those involved directly with the tour. This was very new to me. Usually I just packed up and headed home immediately after a performance, but now I was finding out how the other side of show business worked. After these formalities, we headed off to an Irish pub called Kennedy's on west 57th Street. I'm told that the party continued well into the early hours. This was the final show of an amazing tour and everyone was relieved that it had been such a success... and that we were going home.

We were all in jubilant form and had relished our moment of glory. We listened to speeches from the promoters, the managers and of course Phil himself. Even I made a speech that night!

However, I longed to get home, not just to see my family, but also to give my solo career a shove forward. There were television, radio and press leads that I needed to chase up. But looking back to 1993, I realise that it was the most significant year in my career to date. I learned an enormous amount about performance, rehearsal, behaviour and everything it takes to make a success of touring and performing. We travelled back to Ireland in business class – another first for me. I arrived home on 3rd December, exhilarated and delighted to be back. I had so many stories to tell of my amazing six weeks living and touring in the USA.

Chapter 25
It's Christmas again!

Christmas 1993 was just as busy and exciting as any other in the Fleming household. Mam always started her preparations weeks in advance to make sure that everyone's tastes and needs were catered for. Now as I reflect on Christmas, I see it that it is one of those times when happy emotions can sometimes be tinged with feelings of sadness and loneliness. But I know I will always have my memories of Christmases past. They are a gift that only a Mam and Dad can give you! After the hustle and bustle of the Christmas and New Year celebrations, 1994 was here. I had lots to think about and career plans to make!

Chapter 26
De Dannan

As it happened, I didn't have much time to think about my career direction, as I got a telephone call from Frankie Gavin, fiddle player and leader of De Dannan. He asked me to join the group as lead singer for some of their upcoming UK shows. Eleanor Shanley, their previous singer, had just left to pursue a solo career. This offer meant a lot to me, as every Irish singer that I admired, or had been influenced by, had spent some part of their career with De Dannan. These included Maura O'Connell, Mary Black and Dolores Keane, to name but a few. The list was a 'who's who' of the Irish music industry at the time. I accepted the offer and got ready to leave again.

My first show with De Dannan was in the Royal Concert Hall in Glasgow in mid January 1994. I arrived in Glasgow on the day of the first show and made my way to the venue to meet the band. I had never met any member of De Dannan prior to that day. I had no idea what to expect but I figured my experience with Phil Coulter was enough to get me through this tour. But I quickly found out this was to be a million miles away from how Phil toured. There was little in the way of rehearsals and a somewhat casual attitude about putting the show together. It was also very traditional. I met Frankie and the rest of the gang in the dressing room, and while I was extremely anxious about the content of the show, which was now only four hours away, everybody else was in party mode. I couldn't believe what I was seeing!

I sat down with Frankie and Alec Finn, who played guitar and bouzouki, to work out some songs. We decided the easiest solution would be to choose those songs that the band had recorded with previous singers and that I already knew. All we had to do was change the keys to suit my voice. This was my introduction to *Hard Times*, the song that has almost become anthem with my own shows. For this show, there were to be three groups on the night as part of the Celtic Connections Festival. These included Cherish The Ladies, Dolores Keane and De Dannan. I was to perform five songs to an audience of over 2,000. What a surreal

Ballymun Library Tel: 8421890

feeling! There I was, performing with the most legendary traditional bands in Ireland, and me the lead singer with De Dannan!

There were four shows to fulfill in the UK at venues in Glasgow, Bradford, Manchester and London. Not only was each venue very different, there were also different egos to be massaged along the way, something that's not easy when everyone is crammed into a minibus. The whole experience was a long way from the tour bus in America and the hotels were certainly not similar. But somehow I was okay. I had more say and control over the songs I wanted to sing and while they say 'a change is as good as a holiday' but this was no holiday I can assure you!

When I returned home I had more or less made my mind up not to continue with De Dannan. I had never been fully committed to the band and I'd always had my eye on the prize of going solo. That was until Frankie called me a couple of days later with a proposal. He wanted me to tour regularly throughout the year. The proposal included dates in Australia, Hong Kong, China, Europe, Bahrain and the USA. That was it. My decision was made for me. I would never again get an opportunity to see these countries without being part of a group like De Dannan.

To be fair, the financial perks were also attractive and it was certainly better than trying to sing over the loud hum of a crowded bar full of smoke, noise and the sound of breaking glasses. I had never noticed, or even been bothered by any of this until my concert experience with Phil Coulter and De Dannan, where the audience would cling to your every note and lyric.

Above
De Dannan – Alex Finn, Colm Murphy, Frankie Gavin, Me, John Faulkner, Derek Hickey at The Great Wall of China during a tour.

Below left
Performing with De Dannan in Hong Kong.

Below right
Performing with Aoife Clancy at the Milwaukee Irish Festival 1994.

Chapter 27
Decisions

Above left
A break from touring with
De Dannan while on tour
in Australia.

Above right
In Liz and Des Gallagher's
home in Hong Kong.

Below
Alex, Frankie and Me in
Hong Kong.

It was now March 1994, and Phil Coulter had major plans to record an album. I was asked to attend a studio to record my debut single with him, a song called *Wait Till The Clouds Roll By*. However there were a few disagreements about the arrangement. I felt the key set for the songs was too low and should be changed. The problem was the tracks had already been recorded and couldn't be changed. I was unhappy with the recording and felt I wasn't able to do it justice.

The single was released a month later and this led to another appearance on The Late Late Show. It was to be very different from my first appearance. I performed *The Auld Triangle* with the Voice Squad, with Phil accompanying me on piano. As my debut single, the song was expected to perform well in the charts that week. The performance on The Late Late Show was wonderful and there were no problems with mics or anything else, apart from the fact I was embarrassed by how I looked, dressed like a 19th-century farmer. Phil thought I should dress in this more traditional style. But the look really wasn't me and I was concerned that I might be losing control of my career. Despite my appearance, I thoroughly enjoyed my performance and as it turned out, the single had little or no impact on my career. It got limited airplay and quickly disappeared altogether.

Phil offered me a record deal with his company, Four Seasons Music. Although this was something I had wanted for a long time, I just felt I wasn't ready to accept his offer at that time. I decided to take some time to think about it and went on tour with De Dannan.

During this tour we played throughout France, Holland and Germany during the Spring of 1994 and then on to Bahrain in the United Arab Emirates – the highlight of the tour for me. The weather was the hottest I had ever experienced in my life. On some days it was so extreme I had to stay in my air conditioned hotel all day and not expose my pale Irish skin to such extreme temperatures.

After four days in Bahrain, it was on to Hong Kong. This was an amazing place and topped everywhere we had been so far. We spent a total of five days in this exotic city. Our accommodation had been arranged in advance by the organisers, we would be staying with members of the Irish Society. I was lucky enough to stay with Des and Liz Gallagher, who were originally from the midlands of Ireland. It couldn't have worked out better for me. Des and Liz were not big into the social side of these functions. They were more interested in sight-seeing, culture, music and meals out. My kind of people! I was the youngest of the group and I'd never before seen the countries and cultures we were visiting, so I wanted to experience it all! I certainly didn't intend wasting my free time sleeping. With these two brilliant tour guides to take care of me, I was going to see everything I could in Hong Kong. We performed a one-off show there. The excitement and atmosphere that night were electric! It felt more like a session at home than a concert, everyone had an amazing night and what a great personal achievement to be performing in Hong Kong! The city and its people left an indelible mark on me and they are both still a big part of my life today.

Next it was off to Australia, the most anticipated part of the tour for me. We left on a Friday morning bound for Sydney and when we landed I felt right at home. This wasn't because Australia was similar to Ireland, it was more to do with the weather. We had arrived in June, their winter, and temperatures were around 18 to 19 degrees centigrade – roughly equivalent to an Irish summer. High temperatures aren't my thing!

Chapter 28
Travel weary me

Australia would be our home for the next four weeks. We opened the tour in Sydney and then moved on to Melbourne, Brisbane, Adelaide, Byron Bay and many more venues. Each city was a new adventure, a new experience and a fantastic opportunity to learn. The tour closed in Perth, Western Australia, a small city that reminded me very much of Galway city at home. The last show was quite low key, with a lively crowd who seemed to be there more out of curiosity than as fans of the music. But by that point I'd really had enough and couldn't wait to get home. I was missing my parents, my family and home-cooked Irish food. I didn't go to the closing party because I was completely exhausted and there were over twenty six hours of flying ahead of me.

By this stage, flying was becoming a bit of an issue for me. I had spent so much time in the air over the last eight or nine months that I had begun to worry about my safety every time I boarded a plane. I was particularly anxious before the flight home from Australia, so I rang Mam and Dad to let them know that I was well and would be home soon. They were delighted to hear from me and assured me all would be well with the journey. The candle was still lit at home!

I arrived in London after a gruelling twenty-six hour flight, feeling like I had been shot through a cannon. It was six o'clock in the morning and my flight to Dublin wasn't due to take off for another seven hours. I transferred to the correct terminal, found the cleanest piece of floor and lay down for some much needed sleep. I really didn't care what happened around me. I was so worn out that I just had to lie down anywhere. At last my flight was called and as I boarded the plane home, I started to get excited. My sister Cathy and brother Patrick collected me in Dublin airport and despite the prospect of a three and half hour drive home, I was just so glad to be back on Irish soil and to be heading home to the safety of my parents and a much needed rest. My parents were of course delighted to see me back. There were great celebrations and a special celebratory home-cooked Irish meal. Mam extinguished the holy candle that she'd kept lit since I went on tour and put it away until my next trip.

Chapter 29
My big offer, or was it?

I only had a two week break before I was due to fly back to the USA with De Dannan for the Irish Festivals tour. There was still the issue of the record contract from Four Seasons Music to be dealt with, so I called Phil Coulter and arranged to meet him at his office. My sister Cathy and I travelled to meet Phil. We both knew we had a BIG decison to make and that it would have a serious impact on my career moving foward. During that journey to Wicklow we went through all the pros and cons and no matter how long we discussed it, I couldn't bring myself to accept it.

We informed Phil I would not be signing the contract and looking back, I realise that I probably could have dealt with the situation a little better. But I think the outcome would have still been the same, although I did worry that my decision would affect our working relationship and there was a chance it would now be severed.

The Hong Kong Folk Society

in conjunction with
The St. Patrick's Society of Hong Kong
Present

De Dannan
with singer Tommy Fleming

Monday, 18 March, 1996, 8:00pm
City Hall Theatre
Central, Hong Kong
Tickets $250 / $200 students
Available from All Urbtix Outlets (Tel. 2734 9009)

Since their founding 22 years ago, De Dannan have been at the forefront of Irish music. Featuring two of Ireland's finest talents, Frankie Gavin on fiddle, and singer Tommy Fleming, they present a blend of traditional and contemporary music styles. Don't miss this chance to see one of Ireland's finest bands.

Chapter 30
Off again, more prayers

There were about fifteen festivals booked across the USA for De Dannan, taking in some major cities including Milwaukee, Chicago, New Jersey. I loved touring, but I hated flying! All the same, I had no choice but to get on with it. Flying on long haul and internal flights was part of my job, and I just had to do it.

I was now the full time lead singer with De Dannan, a position I still viewed as temporary, but one I would hold for a further three years. I was also still pursuing my solo dream. During those three years, I recorded the *Hibernian Rapsody* album with De Dannan, which again had little or no impact on the music charts. It featured a cross section of music and singing, and because De Dannan was considered a traditional group, my singing tracks received little if any exposure on TV and radio. Singers tended to be left in the background. So if I wanted to be heard or seen, I would have to fight my corner to get exposure.

During those three years, De Dannan celebrated its 21st anniversary as a group and a celebratory concert was held in a circus big top in Galway City. Any of the previous members who could attend were invited to do so. It was a magical evening, with performances from Mary Black, Delores Keane and of course myself, together with past musicians like Charlie Piggot on banjo, Mairtin O'Connor on accordion and many more. It was three and half hours filled with the very best music and song. But I must admit I felt slightly jealous, watching all the other singers walk away afterwards to resume their solo careers. Once again I felt it was getting near time for me to make a break and follow my own path.

Chapter 31
Going Solo

Left
On stage in Tokyo.

My time with De Dannan came to an end around mid 1996 and I continued to perform solo gigs wherever possible. But when I left De Dannan, I also left a steady income behind me and I slowly started to run out of money. Working as a solo singer meant it was now my responsibility to pay everyone involved in my shows. And somehow this wasn't working out very well. There never seemed to be enough ticket sales to cover the costs of the band and with little or no work coming in, my financial situation was very rapidly becoming rather dire. I desperately needed a manager with the experience and knowledge to sort all of this out.

I had left home by this stage and was living full time in Stillorgan, Dublin. I had initially moved in with my sister Cathy, but what was planned as a short term stay, had turned into months. I later moved to Clonskeagh, sharing a house with two sisters, Valerie and Michelle Mangan. I needed to be in Dublin in order to get my solo career moving forward and onto the next level. But by now I was completely out of money and had to depend on my parents and sisters for financial support. Without their love and support I would have never survived in Dublin. But all was not lost and even though I hadn't a penny, I managed to secure three investors to finance the recording on a new album.

My plan was to record a new album and sell it at gigs whenever I toured. I recorded my debut solo album, *Different Sides To Life*, in July 1996 using a host of musicians I'd met throughout my career. It was around this time that I was introduced to a music manager who was interested in working with me moving foward.

Chapter 32
Touring again - the return

Summer 1996 had come and gone, and with little or no work coming in, I was pretty much surviving on hand outs. This certainly hadn't been my intention, nor was it something I was used to, so I was becoming more and more frustrated, trying to get my career moving. Then out of the blue in September I received a phone call from my old friend Phil Coulter. He wondered if I would be interested in joining him for another tour of the USA, to include an appearance in Carnegie Hall, New York. The pay was good and this time I knew exactly which songs I wanted to perform and how they should be arranged. We finalised the deal and soon I was off to the USA again for almost six weeks.

We opened the tour at the Boston Symphony Hall, and as before, the audience was amazing. Indeed, this was how things continued throughout the tour. Our final appearance was in Carnegie Hall, but this time I was ready and with so many tours now under my belt, I knew how to prepare properly and avoid any mishaps. There was one surprise however. It was announced that there would be an additional guest for the New York show. Liam Neeson was to make a special guest appearance.

So there I was, waiting side stage before being called and who should be standing next to me but Liam himself. I was completely in awe of him. Not only was he a major box office movie star but his physical presence alone was enough to intimidate anyone. Phil introduced me on to the stage and I sang the *Isle Of Inisfree* and *Danny Boy*, both of which went very well. As I left the stage I received a standing ovation. Phil then introduced Liam, who was to recite *Coney Island*, a song and poem written by Van Morrison. When he walked on stage after me to perform his piece, he said, "How do I follow that? I hope he doesn't take up acting". I couldn't believe what Liam Neeson had just said about me. What a wonderful endorsement from such a successful man. It was just the confidence boost I needed at the time. I was no longer the innocent twenty two year old who arrived on the first USA tour with Phil. I was now a twenty five year old with attitude! Phil and I exchanged artistic differences a number of times during the tour, however they haven't stopped us from working together on several other projects throughout my career to date. The USA tour finished close to Christmas and I returned home with a little money in my pocket. Mind you, it wouldn't last long in Dublin.

Chapter 33
My biggest mistake

After an exhausting tour, we had a few days off in New York before returning to Ireland. I fully intended to enjoy myself, do some Christmas shopping and take in some of the sights. To my total shock I got a surprise visit from the music manager I'd been introduced to back in Dublin. He met me in the Fitzpatrick Manhattan hotel and made his move to secure himself as my manager by producing a contract to manage my career. Against all advice and genuine concern from family and friends, I signed it! I was clutching at straws and was desperately looking for help to get my career on track, fast. I believed it to be a five year contract but it turned out to be for ten years, locked in. I very quickly realised that this was the biggest mistake of my life, although it was at least four years after I'd signed the contract before I could finally admit it.

Chapter 34
Another Christmas

Christmas of 1996 was once again a special get-together for all the family. Mam and my sisters really pulled out the stops to make it an especially enjoyable one for everybody. I was due to be at home in Sligo for about three weeks and after a very hard touring schedule and a year of serious financial worries, I was very much looking forward to spending time at home in the comfort of my old bedroom. I was able to relax at home, and felt quite confident that everything was going to work out fine, now that I had a manager. I guess it was the safe feeling we get when we are secure at home, the place where you go to heal your hurt.

Around mid January, I went back to Dublin and set about trying to secure some more work, even though the new manager was now on board. Things were at a complete stand still, with no prospects on the horizon. There were only a few odd gigs here and there, with little or no money. Even when I did make a profit, the money went towards the manager's percentage. I was in a vicious circle. Whenever we played a number of gigs together, all the musicians and engineers got full rate, and any profits had to go towards the losses incurred by previous gigs. I had convinced myself that things would get better once I had a manager to look after my career – I could concentrate on singing and leave business matters to him. That wasn't how things were working out. The situation was spiraling out of control. Fast!

Leabharlanna Poibli Chathair Bhaile Átha Cliath
Dublin City Public Libraries

Chapter 35
Time to be creative

It was around this time in Dublin that I met the singer/songwriter, John Hurley. We worked together doing small shows in the Dame Tavern on Dame Street and at Whelans on Wexford Street. John and I performed well together and I felt quite at home with him. In John, I felt I'd finally found a song writer who understood my singing style and had a grasp of how I wanted to deliver my music. With so many disappointments in my life at that time, meeting John provided a welcome creative break and it was a time that I enjoyed very much.

Then at last I got the break I'd been looking for. I was invited to be part of a compilation album to celebrate the music of Jimmy McCarthy, composer of such songs as *No Frontiers*, *Katie* and *Bright Blue Rose*. I would feature alongside a number of legendary Irish singers, including Christy Moore, Maura O'Connell, Mary Black and others. I was asked to record *As I Leave Behind Niedin*, a lament to Kenmare in County Kerry, and, contrary to what many people think, is not about a woman called Niedin. I was delighted to be included in such a high profile project and couldn't wait to get it recorded and released.

The studio was booked and the session was due to start at 8.00am on a Wednesday morning. I arrived around 7.30am, full of enthusiasm and ready to go, but no one else showed up until 9.00am. This surprised me a little but it didn't really matter as it gave me time to settle into my surroundings. The song was produced by fiddle player, Maire Breathnach, who still appears on many of my albums. The song featured a piano, double bass and Maire herself on fiddle and viola. The recording session lasted about five hours, with vocals being the last piece of the jigsaw to be completed. I sang the track over and over and even when I thought we had a great vocal recording, Maire would point out a few flaws and send me back to do it again. I was amazed at her knowledge of the recording process and I learned more in that one day than I had in the previous three years. My experience with Maire instilled in me a commitment to professionalism that has helped me to deliver many more albums throughout my career.

In September of 1997, Tyrone Productions filmed a number of concerts in Dublin's Point Theatre for a television series called Gaelforce. These concerts featured the best in Irish music from the Chieftains, Clannad, Christy Moore and many more. De Dannan were included in the line up and and they invited me to join them for their performance. Former singers Mary Black and Maura O'Connell also joined in on the night and the show culminated in a finale in which the three of us performed *Hard Times* together. It was filmed for TV and recorded for release on CD and DVD. The series was broadcast on RTÉ television later that Autumn and after its release, the CD reaching number five in the Irish album charts. This provided a huge boost to my career and, most importantly, to my self esteem, which had taken a severe battering of late, both from the lack of work and, but more so from the lack of enthusiasm shown by those around me.

Once again I had to become the architect of my own success. I worked hard to book some shows on the back of Gaelforce's success, but I always faced the same dilemma. I couldn't book a show without my manager's consent and if he finally agreed to the show, the venues would either be booked out, or the musicians I needed would be unavailable. It was a complete and utter disaster. Things had become so bad financially that I had no choice but to apply for social welfare assistance to try to keep living in Dublin.

In early December of that year, *Warmer For The Spark*, the Jimmy McCarthy tribute album, was released to great success. It reached number three in the Irish album charts and despite this being another fantastic opportunity to propel my career forward, in my opinion it was neither exploited nor developed by those who were supposedly looking after my career. There were no TV, press or radio interviews, in fact it was as if I didn't even feature on this album. When I challenged those concerned about this apparent lack of follow up, the excuses ranged from, "The DJ's don't know who you are" to "The journalists only want to interview well known artists".

I argued that unless my name was pushed out there, the press would never know about me! My pleas seemed to fall on deaf ears, to the point that I almost became convinced that they were right and that I shouldn't be pushing so hard. I felt their reaction was, "Oh! It's just Tommy, so don't heed what he has to say". As I say, I almost agreed with them, but never fully!

The Friday night spot on RTÉ was held by Kenny Live. It was presented by Pat Kenny and while similar in style and content to The Late Late Show, had more emphasis on music. The final show of 1997 was scheduled a week before Christmas and was to be a tribute to Jimmy McCarthy. Almost all the artists who had sung or played on the *Warmer For The Spark* album were due to appear, with individual performances by Mary Black, Maura O'Connell, Mary Couglan, Frances Black and little old me. I'd been pushing hard for something like this to be arranged and I was delighted to be included. Suddenly here I was once again on television. I believed this was going to kick things off.

The show went well and the celebrations continued on into the early hours. Perhaps I was finally making some headway on my path to solo success! It seemed so, because shortly afterwards I was offered a solo recording contract. This was my dream. I felt it, I believed it, and I was nearly there.

I made my way back home to Sligo for another Christmas with my parents and family. I couldn't wait to tell them my good news – I had secured a record deal with DARA Records, one of the most successful independent labels in Ireland! Maybe now all my years of struggling would be over. It was a great Christmas and New Year celebration. Things were well and truly on the up.

Above
My Kenny Live performance.
Left-right Marie, Pat Kenny, Joanne Fleming, Cathy, Me and Belinda.

Below
Cathy, Jimmy McCarthy and Me at Kenny Live.

Chapter 36
My final release

I was now full of creative ideas about what I would like to record on my second studio album. I desperately wanted to include original songs, as I believed this would give it more credibility. Fortunately, I had access to the writers I needed to achieve this. I had already worked with John Hurley over the previous two years and had built up an array of material with him. I had also been introduced to a writing duo from the USA called Lowen and Navarro, as well as a writer similar in style to John Hurley called John Gorka. They all had material that was suitable for me and I wanted it to feature heavily on the new album. But numerous rows ensued about what would feature on this album. I wanted to use the recent songs, while those around me wanted me to cover more Celtic sounds. The term Celtic embraces a number of countries including Ireland, Scotland, Wales and northern France, but others seemed to believe that 'Celtic' was synonymous with 'Irish'. Needless to say, I desperately tried to ignore this interference, though everything was done to upset the momentum of the recording. Momentum is critical to a recording. It is the essential element that delivers the all important 'feel' of an album, imparting passion to the recordings and heart to the songs.

Restless Spirit was born. Recording started in early March, with the first single released in April, called *Through a Child's Eyes*. After its release an advertising and publicity campaign which included radio interviews, press editorials and many public appearances was set up for me. The more I could do the better. I was determined to get my name out there. The release date for *Restless Spirit* was set for early October. However, every week there appeared to be yet another reason as to why the album should not be released on schedule. The excuses ranged from not been able to secure proper positioning in major record chains, or making sure we had a confirmed appearances on TV shows like The Late Late Show or Kenny Live, to ensuring the album got the proper promotion it deserved. Finally the release date was agreed for the last Friday in October 1998.

I was so looking forward to the album hitting the shops and I truly believed this would be the making of my career. Everything was in position to make it a big seller. Everyone was behind it to ensure its success.

Chapter 37
The day I thought my career and my life were over

Above
On the street of Aclare shortly after the accident.

Below left
What was left of the white Volkswagen Golf after the accident.

Below right
My Jerome Halo Brace.

One week after its release, *Restless Spirit* was number three in the charts. Now it was time to really pull out all the stops and get on the road to promote the album. As this was my first release with the record company, I had yet to prove myself, so I wasn't in a position to make any demands. I just wanted the album to sell and prove to everyone I had a career in music, so I was prepared to do anything, absolutely anything, to make sure that happened.

An intensive two and half week long promo trip was organised, but neither the record company nor management could provide a driver or a personal assistant to help me as budgets just weren't available. It meant visiting three to four radio stations per day, taking in press interviews and personal appearances in every shopping centre, record store and anywhere I could pitch my stand. I had to travel all over Ireland but I firmly believed I could do all of this myself, and do it successfully, so that the album would work for everyone involved.

On the 26th November 1998, I was proved tragically wrong. I was on my way home from a gruelling promo trip which had taken in visits all over the South of Ireland, I had already driven over one hundred and fifty miles that day to get back home and I stopped in Ballina to meet a friend for a while. Afterwards I set off on the remaining fifteen miles to my parents house. But by now the effects of fatigue were really kicking in. Shortly after midnight, about three miles from home, I fell asleep behind the wheel of my Volkswagen Golf and drove head on into a tree. I was shocked but conscious after the initial impact and I realised the car was on fire. The door wouldn't open but somehow I managed to get free by pushing myself through the window. I desperately tried to get away, and by walking and crawling, I eventually managed to drag myself about thirty yards from the wreck. Just as I did the car exploded! I sat on the side of the road in complete darkness, and in a complete state of trauma. I knew I had a broken wrist and possibly a few other broken bones, as well as cuts and bruises. I also believed I had whiplash as I had a severe pain in my neck. After sitting watching my car and my belongings go up in smoke, there was nothing for it but to try to and make my way home. There I was, sitting on a back country road, looking at a burning car, with no house for miles. Plus facing the possibility that no one would be along the road for hours.

I started making my way home, carefully picking my steps along the road, and after what seemed like an eternity, realised I'd only managed to walk about a mile. Suddenly car headlights appeared as a neighbour drove towards me and stopped. I was never so glad to see anyone in all my life! Shock was setting in and I don't recall much about the journey home but I know he got me into his car and drove me back to Mam and Dad's. When I got to the back door I realised I had no keys, they were still in the burning car. I called out several times and eventually my sister Belinda came down and opened the door. I was so relieved to be home, I honestly didn't realise how broken up I was until Belinda sat me down and tried to clean me up. I had a six inch gash on my forehead just above my hairline, there was congealed blood all over my face and shirt and I had a severe pain in my neck and chest. Eventually Belinda convinced me I needed to get to hospital to be checked out. I just wanted to go to bed and rest as I was exhausted and feeling really sorry for myself. But she wouldn't take no for an answer and drove me to Castlebar General in County Mayo, about twenty five miles from home. I was sure I would only need a few stitches and maybe a plaster on my wrist. Then I'd be sent home again as soon as they patched me up. How wrong I was!

When we arrived I was seen immediately and subjected to all sorts of tests, from vision reflexes to X-Rays. There seemed to be a slight sense of panic about all the attention I was getting, and that made me begin to panic a bit too. Something wasn't right. I soon discovered just what was wrong! I had a broken neck!

By this stage, word had reached the rest of the family and Cathy and Patrick had arrived at the hospital. They were all waiting anxiously for an update when the Doctors who had diagnosed the neck fracture told my family that I needed to be taken to the spinal injuries unit in the Mater Hospital in Dublin and that I would have to go immediately. I would be taken by ambulance as the weather was unsuitable for the air ambulance, particularly with this type of spinal injury. They also said they couldn't assess the full extent of the damage until I'd had more tests and MRI scans in Dublin, so the sooner I got there the better.

It was now around 3.00am and my sister Cathy and a nurse travelled with me to Dublin. I will never forget the pain of the injury and the hard plastic collar that pressed painfully into my skull throughout the journey. It took about four hours, mainly because of the low speed the ambulance had travel at, as any bump or movement could have destabilised the fracture, leading to complete paralysis. We arrived at the Mater Hospital around 7.00am and I was assessed again. Eventually when the doctors and nurses had completed their assessments, examinations and X-Rays, I was transferred to the spinal injuries unit. I was completely terrified at this stage and would have done anything to get myself up and out of there. I felt so helpless and everything around me seemed completely out of my control.

All I was aware of was surgery, more tests, and lots of waiting. I was constantly asking questions, only to be told that "I didn't need to worry about that now". I knew the specialist in charge had taken my sister Cathy to a private room for a chat. That was bad. I knew it must be something serious if he couldn't say what was wrong in front of me. When Cathy returned, she said everything was fine and not to worry. Honestly, if one more person told me not to worry, I was going to lose it. Afterwards, I found out she had been told just how serious the injuries were and that there was a possibility of paralysis, even if I did have surgery. I only found this out several weeks later when I was well into recovery.

When Cathy came back from speaking to the consultant she said I had two options. The first, and the most likely to fix the fracture, was an invasive procedure where they would make an incision under my Adam's apple at the front of my neck to attach two one-inch pins onto the two broken vertebrae. The other option was to attach a large brace to my head which would be screwed into my skull in six places. This would be attached to a fiberglass casing around my torso in order to secure my body from the shoulders up. There were no guarantees that either of these procedures would work. Plus, if I went for the brace, I would have to wear it for at least six weeks before they could tell if it was working. After much deliberation and serious panic attacks, I finally choose the brace. The invasive procedure carried the risk of severing my vocal chords. So that definitely wasn't an option!

Eventually I was taken to the operating theatre for surgery. While I was semi-conscious they attached what is known as the Jerome Halo Brace. This involved making incisions into my skull and drilling holes where the screws would secure the brace to my head. To say I was scared as hell is an understatement. I was begging God to get me through this and praying that I might fully recover... or die. I truly had no fear of dying. My worst fear was paralysis.

When the procedure was completed and the brace had been fully attached to my head, I was transferred to recovery and then to the main ward where I stayed for the next five days. As I lay in that bed feeling sorry for myself, all I could think about was that all the hard work I had done was completely wasted. I was told that I would not be able to work for at least 18 months and certainly not tour for at least two years. I was devastated. Concerts had been booked in major venues throughout the country, plus I was in the middle of my first major promotion tour for the release of *Restless Spirit*. I couldn't believe this was happening.

Everything but everything that I had worked for was gone in one second. After a week in the Mater Hospital's spinal unit, I asked to be discharged, as I felt I would recuperate better in the safe, secure surroundings of home. The doctors were against the idea, but I kept the pressure on, begging them to let me return home. They eventually conceded as long as I did everything they advised, which was rest, rest, rest! Cathy collected me on the Friday morning but it was the afternoon before I was discharged. I had to use a wheelchair to get to the car park and that's where the fun and games started. I wasn't used to wearing the frame on my head and body, so I found myself losing my balance every time I took a step forward.

By the time the nurse and Cathy eventually manoeuvred me into the front seat of the car, it was almost an hour later. I had orthopedic pillows all around me and behind my head. The seat was fully reclined to make space for me and the brace, which seemed to have become twice its size since leaving the hospital ward. At last we were on our way. The three hour journey home was a mixture of conversation and sleep.

Of course, the conversation was all about my future, or lack of it, and what I was going to do if or when I recovered. Cathy was great, constantly reassuring me that it would all work out fine. I needed to focus on getting better. All the same, I was extremely apprehensive as to how my Mam and Dad would react, as they had not seen me since the accident. I wouldn't allow them to see me in the spinal unit. I knew they were both crazy with worry and I felt it would be far too upsetting for them to travel to Dublin and see me lying in the hospital. I made sure they were only told the bare minimum of information and that they were reassured I was going to be fine. My family explained to them that I would look a lot worse than I actually was, that the cage was necessary and not to panic. I also knew that once I was home, Mam would take care of me, so I was looking forward to getting home and closing the door on the world outside.

We arrived at home around 7.00pm. I was overwhelmed with joy and apprehension at the prospect of walking through the front door. Cathy insisted on trying to help me but I was having none of it. I was going to walk through the door by myself so that Mam and Dad would see me as an independent man, and not as a broken and helpless patient. Mam greeted me as soon as I walked through the front door and I saw her eyes fill with tears as she reached out to help me through the hallway. I shrugged off any help and explained that I was going to be fine and not to cry... to which she said they were tears of joy and that she was just glad I was home. My poor Dad just took one look at me and headed outside. I knew his heart was breaking. No matter how much I pretended everything was fine, I knew they could see right through me and everyone was fighting back the tears. Mostly me.

That night was one of the happiest I ever spent with my family. The tea flowed and my Mam filled me in on all the phone calls, letters and cards she had received, wishing me a speedy recovery. This may have been a rough situation but I could see the pride in her eyes as she told her stories, all the time avoiding the proverbial elephant in the room... my broken neck, my smashed up face, gashed forehead, broken nose and broken wrist and ribs. I was a right mess, in every sense of the word.

For the next six weeks I followed the same daily routine, get up at 10.00am, have my breakfast made by Mam, then sit in the same big armchair and watch TV for most of the day, with Mam checking in on me every hour or so. She was treating me like a delicate piece of china and killing me with kindness. Sometimes I needed to get out for a walk to get some fresh air and be alone with my thoughts for a while. However I couldn't go walking by myself in case I lost my balance, as the cage made my balance very unsteady. A fall might damage the brace and it would have to be replaced or refitted, or worse, rendered irreparable, which was something I dreaded. Three weeks into my recovery I was climbing the walls with boredom. My day was filled with mind-numbing afternoon TV. I watched everything – Oprah, kid's TV, home makeover shows, and every cookery programme ever shown.

One of my biggest problems was that because of the angle my head was placed in the frame, I couldn't read. I also found it very hard to listen to music because it reminded me so much of what I was missing out on and the ruins my career seemed to be in, compared to where I longed to be. I didn't think it would be possible to pick up where I had left off and carry on with my singing career. And besides, I didn't know if I could still sing! What a dark, dismal place to be and there I was, right in the middle of it!

It was while watching a TV show called 'Pet Rescue' that I had the brainwave of getting a puppy for myself. I thought a puppy would be great company and wouldn't feel sorry for me all the time. I asked Mam to check the classified adverts for dogs for sale, or free to a

Above
Sparky.

good home. After much deliberation, I decided on a brown and white Jack Russell cross. A few phone calls later, Cathy and I headed off to collect him in Galway. Suddenly I had something other than myself to focus on and my depression started to lift. I couldn't believe how tiny he was. I fell in love with him from the moment I picked him up, he was the best distraction I could have had. Sparky and I became best mates and we shared deep conversations about all my worries from that moment on.

After six weeks it was back to the Mater Hospital for a check up to see if the fractures were healing. The X-Rays and MRI scan results showed that there was a significant improvement in the fractures and the brace was working well. But it was going to be slow. I had myself convinced before the results that the doctors were going to tell me all was fine and the brace could be removed. Of course this wasn't the case. I had another six weeks to endure before the brace could come off. To be honest, by that stage I was getting used to wearing the brace and I even ventured outside occasionally for short walks with Sparky. Whenever I headed out for a walk, my poor Mam would sit at the window watching and waiting for me to return. She fretted and worried about my insistence on trying to get some sense of independence back in my life.

I tried to be upbeat and positive about wearing the brace, but this was near to impossible most of the time. I couldn't sleep without taking sleeping tablets, and they made me quite depressed. If I had a few drinks I would also be in a dark place the next day, so no matter what I did I couldn't win. Eventually I found all of my solace in music. I would take my personal CD player to bed and listen to CDs until I eventually fell asleep. Music was the only way I could get through this.

I made another return trip to the my specialist in Dublin and once again I came home bitterly disappointed. I had to wear the brace for a further four weeks. I felt he was being overly cautious, but I had to follow his advice, as he knew best.

Finally, on the 6th March 1999, after seventeen weeks, the brace that had saved my life and given me the use of my limbs, was removed. I can't possibly explain the joy I felt that day. I knew there were going to be a lot of tough times ahead for me regarding my career, as I was starting from the beginning again, but I didn't care as long as I could walk and be healthy. The rest I could work out in time. Things looked good, especially considering how they might have been. One of the first things I did when I got home was have the longest shower ever. I could only take baths while the brace was on.

While I was in the shower, I decided to try and sing. My voice had returned!

Chapter 38
Back to work!

Left
Promoting Acquired
Brain Injury Ireland.

By June 1999 I was back in the studio recording my third album, *The Contender*. For this album I went back to my roots and recorded an album of Irish classics – songs like *Danny Boy* and *The Vale Of Avoca*, as well as contemporary songs by the best Irish writers like Jimmy McCarthy, John Hurley and Christy Hennessey. As positive as I tried to be with the new album, I had to face one disagreement after another with the usual people around me. Their idea of good songs and mine were poles apart, so I had to battle and stress every day to be allowed to do the recording the way I wanted.

After many months in the studio I took some time off for Christmas and the Millennium celebrations. I celebrated the New Year at home with my family and friends. I remember how Mam and Dad were so happy at that new year celebration. All their children, grandchildren and everyone they cared about were together under one roof. Everyone was in good health and they celebrated with such pride and joy that it is only now I realise the gift they gave me that night. It was the gift of memories and happy thoughts, a gift that's invaluable in life.

After Christmas I had to return to Dublin so I could complete the album. I still hadn't received any payments for the album and by now I was completely broke. But I felt I wasn't in a position to complain. So much had been lost after the car accident that I thought if I didn't finish this album, I could kiss goodbye to my singing career. The situation was so bad I didn't even have enough money for petrol or toll bridge charges. I was living on my wits, borrowing money from friends to get me through the week until I was paid. I couldn't afford to rent any accommodation so I had to stay with my close friend, Kathy Cullinan, for weeks on end, while I drove to and from the studio at Stamullen in North County Dublin.

While recording, I developed a strong connection to the songs I'd chosen for this album and I wasn't going to deviate from that path. I recorded thirteen songs in total for *The Contender* album, each song unique and special. They included *Hard Times*, which I had sung with De Dannan, only this time David Hayes put our own stamp on it by adding drums, percussion, pipes, whistle and fiddle. I even had my brother Pat and close friend Ciaran doing backing vocals.

To my mind, it sounded brilliant, but those around me as usual had other ideas. None the less, I stood my ground on this issue until they knew there wasn't going to be a change of heart. *The Contender* was released on Friday, 13th April, 2000 and reached number two in the Irish album charts. It would later chart at number six in the world music charts in the USA.

Chapter 39
Enough is enough!

Later that year I followed the release of the album with an Irish tour. It was very successful, with large attendances, but the costs of staging the show far outweighed the income from ticket sales. So yet again I was back to the usual situation, no money. This continued for over a year, until I finally put my hands up and said ENOUGH!

My career had fluctuated up and down for many months and I was to blame for allowing the situation to continue and get worse. I had a brilliant selling album, decent tours but no money! Everyone close to me tried to advise me but I just didn't know what to do or where to start dealing with the problem. I now realise that I was actually afraid of dealing with all the problems, because for the first time in my life I had no idea how to sort them out.

Suddenly a life line was thrown my way by John O' Shea from GOAL. This Irish aid agency has given relief to some the most poverty-stricken countries in the world. I was asked to perform at a state function at Dublin Castle in honour of the Ugandan President, Musavini, hosted by President Mary McAleese. I sang three songs at the function and afterwards John O'Shea invited me to sit with him and his guests. We chatted for ages about music, favourite songs, artists and during this conversation he asked me would I be interested in raising funds for GOAL with a concert or whatever I thought best. When I explained that I would be better at raising awareness for GOAL rather than trying to raise funds, he agreed and said he would be in touch.

A week later I received a call from John asking me if I would travel to Calcutta with a film crew to participate in a documentary shoot for GOAL. I jumped at the chance and started my preparations for the trip. I had to get about ten injections for all the diseases I might pick up. After I had been given all the shots, John changed his mind and decided to send me to Sudan in central North Africa. So, ten different shots later, plus a week's training with APSO and I was ready to embark on my journey. It was 9th September 2001.

It took a couple of weeks for me to get organised, as I would be away for at least four months to a country I had only ever read about. I had often dreamed of going to Africa and now it was a reality. My parents' reaction wasn't so positive. They thought I was mad, as did my sisters and brothers. But I knew I had to do this. I had committed to it and I felt that if I pulled out now, I would never again see anything through to the end. I also knew that I needed to be far away from Ireland and from everyone in my work circle. Where I was going, no one could reach me, not the manager or the record company... nobody! This was one place that I could escape and be 'me' for a short while. I also had to figure out how deal with every issue in my life that had become a stone in my shoe... and a very painful stone at that.

Left
Unloading supplies off plane in Sudan. I'm counting the bags of grain.

Chapter 40
My biggest, biggest mistake

After another soaking of holy water and another candle lit, I left for Dublin in the afternoon of 8th September 2001. I was staying in the The Great Southern Airport Hotel. I checked in and met David Hayes and his wife Audrey, plus another friend from school, Trisha Buckley. We all enjoyed a bit of chat and laughter until my manager showed up. He wanted me to sign a record contact with him and his company.

My previous record label had not renewed their option for further recordings. I tried to explain that I had no time to look over the contracts and would sign them on my return. But he was having none of it and insisted I should sign them before I left. He made the point that he would start working on new projects while I was away, so that my career could move forward and I would make some money when I came back.

I reluctantly and stupidly signed the contract that would become the focus of a major legal battle a few years later. I knew the minute I signed it that I had made a huge mistake but tried to put it to the back of my mind and concentrate on where I was heading and what that would be like.

Chapter 41
Africa! My love!

Left
Sudan – Africa.

The next morning I boarded the flight for Amsterdam and from there I was bound for Nairobi, Kenya, in Africa. I arrived in Nairobi at 9.00pm, exhausted and apprehensive about what was in store for me. After I collected my bags and headed through passport control and customs, I was met by a couple from Cork, Tom and Toni McCaul, who welcomed me warmly and made me feel instantly relaxed and happy. As we chatted in the taxi on our way into Nairobi, I was completely blindsided by all there was to see in this city. I was particularly struck by the appalling level of poverty inflicted on so many people and the terrible infrastructure as we drove into the city.

I quickly realised there were no rules of the road. Drivers just did what they liked. It was a very frightening experience and I felt most uncomfortable being a passenger in a car with an out-of-control taxi driver, particularly given my own recent experience of car wrecks. There seemed to be no rules for anything, just complete and utter chaos. We finally reached my accommodation, known as the GOAL house. This was where everyone who worked for GOAL stayed until they left for their final destination. I spent two nights in Nairobi. On the morning of 10th September I was due to fly out to Sudan but the flight was cancelled due to inclement weather. As a result I would have to spent another night filled with thoughts and worries, most of which seemed to be saying; "What the hell am I doing here? This is madness".

Around 3.00am, I had my first encounter with mosquitos. By 4.00am my room was like London smog with all the spray I had used to exterminate them. But it was too late. They had got their way and I was bitten all over!

The following morning, I was ready to head off on the next leg of my journey when I heard on the TV news that a plane had crashed into the North tower of the World Trade Centre in New York. I couldn't believe what I was looking at when I watched in horror as the second plane crashed into the South tower. By now, everyone from the offices above was in the living room, watching the television in disbelief as the 9/11 attacks unfolded live on TV. This was the first time I had ever heard the name 'Bin Laden'. I had to leave and make my way to Nairobi International Airport to catch a flight to Lokichokio, a small town in the Turkana district North West Kenya. This was the nerve centre for all Non Government Organisations, or NGOs. My flight was on a supply plane that flew out to famine sticken regions across Africa.

When I arrived at the airport the level of security had tripled since my arrival three days previously. It was totally intimidating and for a split second I wished that I was at home, not thousands of miles away, heading into the unknown. It was clear from what was happening in the airport that the world had changed forever and travelling would never be the same again. I finally made my way through the mass of people, most of whom were attempting to travel without a passport, which apparently was quite possible in Nairobi, if you had enough money.

I boarded a tiny plane, which made me even more terrified. I then endured one of the bumpiest plane rides ever, and as we came into land, I realised there wasn't even a proper runway or airport in sight, just a hard sand track. I knew that civilisation was further and further behind me and I was truly frightened of what I was facing. I also knew that everyone at home, particularly my parents, would be in a panic, as I hadn't been in touch due to the delays with my travel plans.

We eventually landed in Lokichokio where I had to wait for a few more hours before I would make my final connection to Sudan. I decided to find a satellite phone and I thought my best bet would be in the UN compound. Fortunately, I got the use of a phone line, so I rang home to let my Mam and Dad know I was ok. The connection was a little distorted and there was a continuous crackly sound on the line, so I had to shout down the phone to tell Mam I was in Lokichokio and let her know I was fine. She replied: "That's wonderful, you'll have a great time there." I couldn't figure out how she could imagine I would have a great time in Lokichokio, and besides, I was only going to be there a couple of hours. A few weeks later I found out the reason she had responded so positively. When I said 'Lokichokio', my Mam thought I had said 'Tokyo'. Apparently she had rung everyone and told them I was in Tokyo!

I found my pilot, a guy called Lucas, who was to take me to Sudan in his supply plane, another two seater. After takeoff I noticed we were flying very low so I asked Lucas why this was. His reply scared me stiff, "We need to stay under the radar to avoid being shot at". By now all my notions of playing the starring role in Indiana Jones had been taken over by prayers. I never prayed so hard in all my life. I prayed that we would land safely and I promised myself that I would never complain about trivial things ever again.

When the wheels of the two seater plane touched down on the dusty hot track in Southern Sudan, I could not wait to get off this small plane. Mind you, at the same time, part of me wanted to stay on and beg Lucas to bring me back immediately. I couldn't believe where I was or what was in front of me. There were hundreds of local people out to greet our arrival. As I opened the door of the plane I couldn't decide whether I had arrived in heaven... or in hell. Ironically, after I had spent some time in Sudan, I flew to and from Lokichokio several times without the slightest worry.

Once off the plane I heard a familiar Irish accent. A guy called Jason called out my name a couple of times, then pulled me from the crowd and into a 4x4 to take me back to the camp in Bar el Gazal in South Sudan. I was never so glad to meet a fellow Irishman and another red head, especially in what seemed like such a crazy place. Once safely in the jeep, we headed off, followed by two more 4x4s loaded with supplies from Lucas's plane. My mind was now in overdrive and I was asking questions galore. Where exactly are we? How far to the camp? Are there snakes? Is the camp secured? What happens if I get sick?

Jason was extremely patient. He just kept his cool and answered everything I asked, even though his head must have been fried. Twenty minutes later we drove into the camp which was an enclosure surrounded by a large fence, with two enormous steel gates at the entrance. A huge tree stood in the middle, providing a large area of shade. There were five mud huts and one main building made from galvanised steel. This was the office, clinic, kitchen and dining room. There was dust everywhere.

Jason showed me to my quarters, a single mud hut with a tiny door and window. It had a straw roof and a tiny hand-made bed with a goat skin mattress, two blankets, a pillow and an under sheet. The toilet was a small galvanised structure with a wooden seat. Underneath it was a four-metre hole dug out of the ground, which would be filled back in when it reached a certain level. Our shower was a black tank with a pipe emerging from the base and attached to a watering can nozzle. It was as basic as you could find, but effective.

I was introduced to the other team members at the camp, Jason from Galway and Collin from Kenya. Jason told me he was returning to Ireland and would be leaving me in charge in a week's time, so I had to get up to speed quickly!

One of my abiding memories of that time was when night crept in. A slight coolness returned after the scorching heat of daytime, the dust would settle and the frogs would venture out. Hundreds of frogs would suddenly appear all over the camp. The first time I saw this I was completely creeped out, but after a few days I got used to them and they didn't bother me at all. After a very short time in the camp I felt more safe and secure, and even though each day brought new challenges, I was loving every minute of it. The day came for Jason to leave and although I only had only known him for a week, I felt like we were old friends. I dreaded him leaving me here. Part of me wanted to go with him but a bigger part wanted to stay where I was. Permanently!

Above left
Lisa O'Shea, Elisha from Kenya and Me working in camp in Sudan.

Above right
My new home.

Below left
Jason from Galway with Me in the Jeep.

Below right
GOAL Camp shower.

The supply plane arrived, except this time, it was a much larger plane, loaded with a great deal more cargo and many more passengers. I drove Jason out to the airfield and we said our goodbyes but sadness was quickly replaced by excitement as I was to pick up three new recruits, or GOALIES, the name given to us while we worked in Africa. I collected my three very frightened Goalies and introductions were made to Dr. Cathal O'Keefe from Dublin, Louise Hassett from Offaly and Elisha from Kenya. As I drove them back to the camp, it was Louise who had my head fried with questions. "Are there snakes?" "Are there mice?" "Have we any drink for later?" Okay... I made the last one up but I know that's what she was thinking. I answered her questions with the same answers Jason had given me on my arrival. When we got to camp, I gave them the guided tour and explained the do's and don'ts, as well as the general run of things.

That evening we all sat down to a dinner of rice and goat meat, with cans of Tusker beer. We all chatted through the night and got to know each other very well, forming friendships that would last forever. We were to have many such nights, sitting in the silence of Africa with warm breezes blowing around us. After days of hard work and burning heat, the nights were a welcome relief and sometimes we would break the silence by listening to music on a satellite channel called Radio Voyager. It always reminded me of Radio Luxembourg from my younger days.

We spent the next few months together and were as close as a family. We had our own routine, and every day was a tough ride but I was happier than I had been in many years. Each day we travelled out of the camp daily to visit other townlands in the surrounding areas, where we administered food and medicines. Some days we stayed in our own camp where we had a feeding programme for over a thousand children. This was amazing work, the most fulfilling time I had ever spent in my life. During the next few months I would experience peace such as I had never known before. It made a welcome change to my life back home. Here in beautiful Africa there were no deadlines to meet, no one was calling looking

Above
Dining in Africa, Me with Anita Reen and Toni and Tom McCaul, GOALIES.

Below left and right
Working in Sudan.

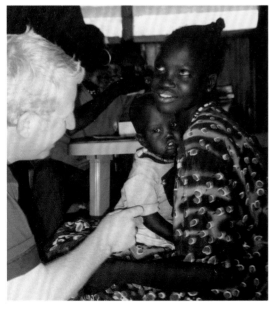

to get paid from money I didn't have, there was no pressure from people I no longer trusted with my career, a career that was almost non existent before I left.

Going to Africa was both the worst and the best decision I ever made in my life. I can honestly say it changed me in so many ways. It taught me courage that I never believed I had, it taught me a humanity that I never believed existed, but most importantly, it taught me an acceptance of every person's flaws, good, bad and indifferent, including my own.

I left Sudan in early December to begin my journey home. I hated the thought of going home but I was missing my family quite a lot and after several months of reflection, I now knew what I had to change and I had the courage to make some big decisions. I said my goodbyes to all the local leaders and the many people I had got to know throughout my time in Sudan. I promised and honestly believed I would see them again and I do intend to return some day soon. I flew back to Lokichokio where I spent the night in the UN compound and the next morning we flew to Nairobi, where I stayed for a further two weeks working in an orphanage in the Kibera Slum, about three miles from Nairobi city centre.

Kibera is the second largest slum in urban Africa, with an estimated population of 500,000 people, most of whom live without such basic services as electricity or running water. The poverty I experienced in South Sudan was nothing compared to this type of poverty. It was much worse here, as the people of Kibera lacked any self sufficiency. Instead, they dependend on crime as their only way to survive. Working in the orphanage was the most disturbing and rewarding thing I ever had to do, and trying to keep focused on my work was extremely challenging. I had to prevent myself from getting emotionally involved in the sheer suffering of these tiny, helpless human beings, these children! They were the strongest, bravest and most courageous humans I have ever met, or am likely to meet in my lifetime. They smiled more than most people, they were always in a positive mood and even though they had nothing, absolutely nothing, all they needed was something to eat. This was the biggest lesson I ever learned in my life and it put everything else into perspective. It let me see the stupidity of focusing on material lifestyles instead of appreciating the simple quality of life and health. I left Africa just before Christmas 2001 and as I said my goodbyes to everyone that I had worked with, my tears started to flow. I cried the whole taxi journey to Nairobi airport and I felt exhausted, rewarded and a sense of total sadness. I promised myself I would return but I also knew it would be long time before I would see Africa again, as I had a big mountain to climb on my return.

Chapter 42
Walking into the lion's den

I arrived back in Ireland with mixed emotions. I felt excited to be home but there was also an emptiness inside me after leaving Africa. I had experienced true happiness and contentment for the first time in my life and I had come to realise that the simpler my life was, the happier I was too. Mam and Dad were delighted to see me home, safe and sound. I felt much more confident in myself and I had a clear idea of how I would deal with the issues that were left outstanding when I went to Africa.

In the new year, I set up a series of meetings with everyone involved in my career and told them exactly how I felt and where I wanted to go from here. In return I got plenty of promises and guarantees and off I went again to try and make my career a success.

Left
Lisa O'Shea and Me
just before my departure
from Sudan.

Chapter 43
More of the same!

Throughout the summer of 2001, just before I left for Africa, I had recorded parts of a new album called *Sand and Water*. I finished this album on my return and worked on the material to get it just right. I believed it was my best work to date, as I had worked with some amazing songwriters and musicians, I was convinced it couldn't fail. When *Sand and Water* was released in April 2002, I was sure it would be the turning point in my career, and with all the assurances I had received at the previous meetings, I was certain this could only be the case.

But immediatly after its release, I realised that little or no publicity had been organised, so once again I was left to carry the can. I promoted the album non-stop but this time around it was twice as difficult. The lack of publicity meant that inevitably the album would fail, and it did! It barely made the top twenty and sales were dismal in the first year. I couldn't believe it. After all the promises, I was devastated. Again!

All the hard work from everyone who worked on the album had been wasted. A nationwide tour followed the album's release in Ireland, as well as three shows in Holland. The tour sold well and things began to look positive. The final Irish date in Dublin's Olympia Theatre played to a sold out audience. The next day I discovered that I had made no money whatsoever and in fact I owed money, due to the high expenses incurred throughout the five-week tour!

Once again I couldn't believe what I was hearing. I asked for the figures to check and recheck but it was no good, I was broke. Even worse, I was in debt, with no income and little or no prospects. There didn't seem much point in continuing. I decided to return home to my parents and I asked if I could stay at home for a while. I knew I didn't need to ask but I had been gone a long time and a lot had changed. Mam and Dad knew there was something wrong, so I decided to explain what was going on, except I only gave them a very edited version. I didn't want them thinking I was a failure, after seeing how proud they had been in previous years. I desperately didn't want to take that away from them, nor did I want to worry them too much.

My time at home was spent weighing up my options, asking myself, "where do I go from here?", "what do I do now?" I tried to sack my manager but I was reminded of my contractual obligations. This had come back to bite me very badly and I had no way out. I had also signed a record contract and it seemed I was up the proverbial creek without a boat or a paddle. So I decided my only option was to try and get a job. I needed to train in something, anything that would help me secure a regular income and possibly, only possibly, allow me to do some small gigs at the weekends. I felt truly defeated!

Chapter 44
Something happened and
I could see hope

On June the 2nd, I was attending the funeral of a friend who had worked as a sports presenter in our local radio station. The funeral mass took place in the Cathedral in Castlebar, County Mayo. I arrived in good time and sat near the back of the church. After a short while, a woman I vaguely knew, who was friendly with my sister, sat in the pew beside me. Her name was Tina. We chatted quietly in our seat and then Tina asked me how I got on in Africa. I explained how great it had been, apart from the snake in my hut, to which she replied, "So there were two snakes in the hut". We both giggled, trying not to be seen or noticed. But in truth I knew something had happened from the moment we said hello.

I sang the *Isle Of Inisfree* at the funeral and afterwards we attended a reception in a nearby hotel. Tina and I spent the entire time together, not even noticing anyone around us. We talked about so much, so easily, that time seemed to pass and I didn't even notice it go. I asked Tina if she would like to go for a drink, thinking she would say no. It was a crazy thing to ask, as I didn't even know if this woman was married, in a relationship or anything. I just ploughed ahead, hoping she would accept the invitation and surprise, surprise... she did. We went to a local pub that we both knew and met up with some friends who were also at the funeral. A few hours later I was making my way to my sister's house in Castlebar and I asked Tina for her number. Being the business woman she is, she gave me her business card. I honestly thought she was out my league. Tina was successful and drove a BMW. I drove a Volkswagen Golf that was on its last legs.

A week later I called her and arranged to meet for lunch, but then I cancelled. It was the usual story – I was broke, so how the hell could I pay for lunch. This happened a couple of times before we finally got to meet a few weeks later. In fact, it was over a month after we first met that I finally plucked up the courage to ask Tina out on an official date. I would never have believed that four years later we would be married.

2002 was a very quiet year for me, with few gigs coming my way. I managed to secure a little work by myself, mostly discrete shows in very small venues from Westport to Clonakilty and over to Waterford. I would take just about any booking and when I performed, I actually enjoyed it. It felt sort of free, plus I was earning enough to keep me in pocket money.

That October I was invited to form part of the entertainment on a trip to the Caribbean with our local radio station. Several other acts were also involved. It was a mixed bag of talent – comedy, country & western and traditional. I had taken part in these trips before, only this time it was far more exotic and luxurious. And as I had never been to the Caribbean before, what had I to lose? This was a chance to get a free holiday and earn a bit of money. I called Tina and told her of the holiday, only to discover she had booked for the ten days after I returned home. Disaster! Two groups were travelling and I was in the first group, Tina in the second. At this point we were at a very early and unknown stage of our relationship and I wondered if it would be too soon to go on holidays together. After much thought I took the plunge and asked Tina to try and change her plans and come on my part of the trip. She agreed and a few weeks later we boarded a flight at Ireland West Airport, Knock bound for the Dominican Republic.

We spent the next ten days together in very luxurious suite with an ocean view. I couldn't believe what I was seeing. It was so beautiful and for the first time in years I was with a person I really cared about. I felt better than I had for a very long time. My personal life was in a great place even though my working life was still a shambles. We spent a magical time there, with boat rides to nearby islands, lazy days lying on white sandy beaches, meals out and long walks. It was heaven! I had to work every second night but was only required to sing six songs with the resident band.

While we were in the Caribbean, my record company was preparing to release a collection album and DVD of the best songs I had recorded over the previous ten years. To be honest,

I had little or no interest in this release, as it had all been done before, apart from the bonus CD, which was a live recording from the INEC in Killarney, County Kerry. It was the first live DVD recording I had ever done and I was quite proud of it.

The album was released while Tina and I were away and on my return I didn't do any TV, radio or press. In my heart I felt that if they wanted the album to succeed then they would have to work for it themselves. And work they did! When we returned from the Caribbean the album had been released for one week and had entered the Irish album charts at number eight. This was a good indication as to what my fans wanted to hear. However my manager didn't share that point of view. Weeks went by and there was still no tour in place. Just the odd small gig here and there, nothing of any substance.

Chapter 45
Seasonal highs... and lows

Left
Tina and Me.

Christmas 2002 arrived and as always, members of my family were busy preparing for the holiday period. I was now spending almost all of my time with Tina, we were now truly and officially together and we loved each other's company. On Christmas day, after all the presents had been opened and the Christmas dinner was well and truly digested, I told my Mam and Dad and family that I was going out to visit Tina and I would see them in a few days! Mam and Dad may have seemed a little surprised that I wasn't spending all of Christmas with my family, but they didn't say anything, although I could see all the eyebrows raised as they all thought "This isn't like Tommy, he must be going soft!"

There was major excitement in the family that Christmas, as the build up to my sister Cathy's wedding got underway. She was the first of my sisters to get married. There was lots of work, socialising with family from overseas, visiting and preparations leading up to the big day. It was truly a celebration, with everyone together for a couple of weeks. I just put my career issues on hold and enjoyed my time with my friends and family. My Mam and Dad were busying themselves in every way possible, and I suppose it was a bitter sweet occasion for them to see the first of their daughters walking up the aisle at this wonderful time of year.

The big day arrived and everyone was running around like bees getting themselves ready for the ceremony. I was the first to leave for the church, as it was my responsibility to make sure the music was in place. Cathy had chosen lots of traditional Christmas carols for the ceremony and there were a few old favourites that I had learned over the years. One song in particular will forever stick out in my mind – *True Companion*, written by Mark Cohn. It's a song about love, companionship and marriage. I had sung it for years, so I thought I didn't need to rehearse it. However, I should have. One line in the song certainly wasn't suitable for a small catholic church in the West of Ireland, but I didn't think of this before I launched into it. The line went, "Then I'll take you home and, with wild abandon, make love to you just like a true companion". Yes, it's really quite innocent, but not when you sing it out loud with passion and the local curate doesn't see it as innocent at all. He just stared at me and all I could do to save my embarassment was pretend it didn't happen and look elsewhere. Then I saw Mam staring at me. I felt about one inch tall and wished the ground would open up and swallow me. I just prayed it would blow over pretty quickly, as all I could do was keep going. It wasn't mentioned again that day but I have been reminded of it often enough ever since.

We rang in 2003 with a sense of relief and joy. All the excitement and preparations for Christmas and the wedding were over. Everyone was back to normal with work and family. But my situation was completely different. I had no idea where or when I was going to be working, which meant little or no income. The situation with my management was now in a crisis. The relationship had broken down completely and it would be impossible to rescue it. Everyday I would phone the office to find out when the next booking was coming up, and there never seemed to be one. I was losing confidence in myself and in everyone who worked with me.

Every morning when I woke, I was swamped with feelings of profound doom and depression. I felt I was trapped in a prison and couldn't escape. I never want to experience those feelings ever again. This shortage of work and missed opportunities continued throughout most of 2003. My only income was from sporadic gigs but these were not enough to pay my bills. At this stage Tina was becoming more and more aware of my financial status, which drove my self worth even further into the ground. Tina now questioned how it was possible to be so busy with what seemed successful album releases over the past few years, but still have no money.

I was too embarrassed to tell her the whole truth about my failing career, so I drip fed her bits of information. Eventually however, I knew I could trust her with the full facts, so I asked her to look at the few records and accounts I had been given. It was such a relief to admit the full extent of my financial trouble to someone, and I knew Tina wouldn't judge me but instead would help me to sort it out. The outcome was the simplest thing of all. Tina decided it had to be fixed. All of it, sorted out, once and for all, and move on from there. We were a team from that point on and little by little, Tina made a plan to sort out this huge financial mess. All I had to do was stick to it. Finally something positive was happening and the relief of dealing with the debts and sorting one problem at a time was immense.

Chapter 46
Another disappointment and a reality check

Left
Performing in St Patrick's Cathedral with John O'Brian on Pipes and Bill Shanley on Guitar.

In October of 2003 the management tried all angles to secure a TV deal with PBS, Public Broadcast Service, in the USA. PBS is one of the most successful TV companies in the States, with over fifty million viewers nationwide. I was told that we would be filming the show in St Patrick's Cathedral, Dublin, in mid-October. The material was to be predominantly Irish songs to appeal to the PBS viewers.

I was told there were only two days for rehearsals. But as I wouldn't be working with my usual full time band, I knew it was going to be impossible to get everything right in just two days! I had over fifteen new songs to learn from scratch and I knew I would need at least a week in rehearsals to familiarise myself with them. For some crazy reason I worked tirelessly to learn the songs and I managed to convince myself that this was the right thing to do. What harm could there be in it?

Tina begged me not to go ahead with the show. She realised that things were hopelessly disorganised and that it would inevitability be a disaster. But I ploughed ahead regardless and did it. I even had to borrow a suit from a friend who owned Aware, a men's clothes shop in Sligo, as the budget for the show wouldn't stretch to making sure I was dressed appropriately. Surely that should have been enough of a warning for me to pull out, but no, I was determined to get my career back on track and was willing to try anything. Unfortunately things continued to get worse.

First, I discovered that the lighting engineer wasn't hired until the day before the show. Then it transpired that there was no experienced director to direct on the night and no producer at all to ensure the smooth running of the recording. On the night of the show, Tina travelled with me by taxi from the hotel to the Cathedral, begging me not to go ahead with the recording. I was suffering from a septic throat and flu and was absolutely exhausted. I certainly had some serious doubts about it all, but my loyalty was to the people in the audience who had bought tickets and were now in their seats. I was told that about four hundred tickets had been sold for the event but when I arrived it looked like much more than that. I didn't question it but I never did find out how many people were there. We arrived and I walked in, dressed in my borrowed suit, with a bottle of cough medicine in my pocket to make sure I could get through the songs. I struggled my way through the show, which in my opinion was a complete disaster. I was feeling so ill I kept making mistakes in the lyrics and having to keep repeating them. This was exhausting me even more.

After the show I returned to the hotel and I can honestly say I never felt so low in my life. But I had made up my mind. Regardless of contracts, things would have to change, and soon. I had to fly to Holland the following day to fulfil some concerts, but I promised Tina and myself that that was it, I was going to sort it out. I felt so ill the following morning that I had difficulty getting out of bed, but I had a flight to catch. I asked my manager to get me some medicine, as I had no money. After all, I was performing for nothing. I got the medicine, pulled myself together as best I could and got to Holland. I later found out the cost of the medicine had been deducted from the income from Holland. Imagine my surprise!

Below
On stage in St Patrick's Cathedral.

Chapter 47
Facing my fears

Just before Christmas, Tina and I travelled to meet my manager to deliver the news. The meeting was very short. I simply told him that it was over and I was out. His initial reaction was disbelief and he tried to coax me around with promises of upcoming work. But at last he realised I was completely serious. When Tina also made it clear that Tommy was serious about his decision, we left and I felt an enormous sense of relief that I had finally done it. I knew this wouldn't be the end of the story, but I also knew I was never going to work with him again. Life was just too short!

It was Christmas again and for the first time in years I felt a new sense of energy. I was finally paddling my own canoe again after working with a manager for seven years. I was apprehensive and scared of what lay ahead but I was going to make my own decisions.

Tina and my family were relieved beyond belief that I was taking back control of my career. They knew I hadn't been happy for many years while my career lurched from one disaster to another. They also knew that if I hadn't parted company with the manager, then I might well have lost a lot more than my career, as the stress of the past few years had begun to take its toll on my health.

I spent Christmas flitting between my parents' house and Tina's. We hadn't officially moved in together, or at least that's what we were saying, but my Mam and Dad begged to differ. I knew deep down they were delighted for both of us and they knew that for the first time in years I was truly happy. Our Christmas was filled with socialising, spending time with the kids and helping Santa Clause deliver all the presents. I loved every minute of it.

Christmas and new year seemed to fly past a lot faster than previous years. I had a great deal to organise in the weeks prior to Christmas, as it was now up to me to get work and I intended to do just that. Tina and I started to book some shows for the coming year and with our first one on the 30th January, 2004, there was a lot to do. I had a little knowledge of booking and selling shows from my pre-management days but this was new to Tina. She worked in advertising and media so her background would be a huge benefit. We were determined to make it work and we believed in it totally.

Our first outing was in 120-seat theatre in Manorhamilton, County Leitrim, which was sold out. Everyone travelled to the venue, as we knew we needed all hands on deck to make it work. Plus there was the added fear that the ex-manager might turn up. When we arrived, the theatre manager told us he had received a fax, trying to stop the show, but thankfully he decided to go ahead and allow it to go on. I am still extremely grateful to that theatre manager and his staff for doing so, as they gave me back my professional confidence. Still, the ex-manager's actions showed that he hadn't accepted my decision and was trying as hard as possible to stop my career from moving forward.

Tina, the kids and Pops, my father-in-law, all worked on the night. The concert was a huge success as I was able to sing to the audience and enjoy myself, rather than perform just to keep a manager happy. This was a welcome return to the old Tommy. I felt really positive and upbeat. What's more, something happened that surprised us all – we discovered there was a big demand for my merchandise after the concert. People were queuing up to buy CDs and DVDs from an attractive display we had set up. This was something I had always wanted to have at my concerts, but was never allowed. I got paid for the concert and when we returned home, we couldn't believe how much we had made on merchandise. I felt my independence return, and while we hadn't made a fortune, there was enough to reinvest in the next stage and start paying my bills.

Chapter 48
Onward and upward

Once we got a start, we were off. After years of nothing happening, we were now facing some serious challenges. We needed to move quickly in order to secure bookings in the right venues and we had to get hold of good musicians to deliver the best show we could. We also had to carry all the risks involved with touring but after our first gig experience, we quickly discovered exactly how successful this business could be. Pops made a display for our merchandise by carefully painting my logo onto a large black cloth with white paint and it was ready for the next show.

The next show was scheduled for Castlebar on Valentine's night. We got into promotion mode and started to advertise the concert wherever we could. We would go out at night and distribute posters to all the surrounding towns and villages. We looked after every part of the set up and running ourselves. We hadn't any spare finances to pay anyone to undertake these jobs, so if we wanted to succeed, then it was down to us. This second concert didn't run quite as smoothly as the first one, as the theatre manager bowed to pressure and took a management fee out of what we were paid.

The concert itself was a great success. We had a full band with a proper sound and light system and there was a huge crowd. It turned out to be one of the biggest shows I had ever performed in the West and it certainly was one of the best ever. I was now free to put my own set lists together with David and I could relax more on the stage, and this made for a much better concert for everyone. Also, this was the first night I did a 'Meet and Greet' after the show. I came out to the foyer after the concert and met anyone who wanted a photo, autograph or just a chat. This is something that has continued through the years and is very much part of my show. Believe me, I have met some very interesting and amazing people during these meet and greets.

After Castlebar, we realised we had something that really worked well. I had known all along that this could be a very successful business and there was certainly money to be made. We contacted more venues and booked shows in any theatres that were willing to work with the artist. We were starting to run my career as a business and this involved redesigning everything – posters, flyers and a new website, even though the manager still held the original site. Bit by bit we were starting to build a positive image and a reliable reputation in the business. We concentrated on the one thing that would turn things around and we started to promote, promote, promote.

We did venues of every size, from one hundred seaters to two thousand seaters. The plan was to bring Tommy Fleming to the people and educate them about my music and my performances. I very quickly realised that most of the folk in Ireland's concert venues are brilliant people and without their support at this time I would never have rescued my career. We continued to build a successful business throughout that year, ignoring the correspondence we were receiving. My success meant that some people had realised their Golden Goose had flown and wasn't likely to return. I knew that at some point I would have to deal with this issue, but for now I was busy making a living and enjoying it.

Meet and Greets

This page
Below left
Patrick Hennessy, one of my biggest fans and good friend.

Below right
With Karen Canning, one of my biggest supporters.

Opposite page
Above left
With Dorothy at the Waterfront Hall, Belfast.

Above right
Meeting fans in the Waterfront Hall, Belfast.

Below
INCE Killarney - all the girls.

Chapter 49
A character-building concert!

Above
Rehearsals and sound
checks.

Below left
Building the set.

Below right
Building the stage.

That summer, after working around the country, chatting to the audiences, doing the meet and greets, a thought occurred to me. I believed there was a demand for a special event that would feature the unique music I so much wanted to sing. So I decided to try and organise a concert in the Basilica in Knock, County Mayo. This is one of the most iconic buildings in Ireland and has hosted visitors like Pope John Paul II and Mother Teresa. Knock Basilica is just up the road from my home, so I thought, "Why not try and put a special musical show on in it!" Its concert seating capacity is four thousand, so this would be my biggest concert to date and I was convinced it would be unique.

I contacted the American television company PBS, Public Broadcasting Service, and pitched my idea to them. I spoke to a lady called Diane Bliss who was well known for her success with other Irish artists and groups. She loved the idea and travelled to Ireland to meet us and go through the plan. Diane attended a concert in INEC Killarney in July. She was very impressed and accepted our proposal. When we met her the following day she had a surprising offer for me. She was returning to Ireland in September to attend a recording of a new show scheduled to be broadcast on PBS the following spring, and she asked me if I would co-host the links during the concert as it would be a way of introducing me to the American audience. The show she was returning to record was the first 'Celtic Women'.

We were now well into the summer of 2004, time was moving on and there was much to organise. I had several meetings to secure the venue, and I received a fantastic amount of help and assistance from everyone associated with Knock Shrine. They did everything they could to make it a success. One of the nicest and most gracious people I met during this time was Monsignor Joseph Quinn, RIP, who was introduced to me at my first meeting in Knock. The bond we formed was to help get me through all the subsequent craziness of the build up and performance. He was an extremely gentle, kind, inspiring and understanding person. When permission was finally granted and we were all set to go, I had to promise Monsignor

Joe that we would return the Basilica in the same condition as we found it. He also asked that the music for the concert should be respectful to the building we were going to perform in. *True Companion* certainly wouldn't have worked!

We had no real idea what we were taking on. True, we had learned a lot from doing concerts over the past few months, but this was totally different. In order to get some advice, Tina rang a well know Irish promoter. The only advice she received was, "You're mad". Having gone to the recording of 'Celtic Women' in the Helix, Dublin, we had seen the amount of set up involved in recording a concert of that size. Both Tina and I left that concert very concerned and slightly panicked.

Our challenge was to organise the complete show, get the set designed and build a stage that would suit the Basilica. The building is circular, so it was vital that the set would allow all of the audience to see the stage. We also had some serious lighting issues, as the lights used for TV or DVD are much bigger and totally different to those used for concerts. When I met Alan Nolan in Knock to discuss the sound system requirements, he just stood in the middle of the building shaking his head and looking all around. There was nothing to hang speakers on, a scaffold would have to be built from the ground up, and the speakers hung on it to make sure they worked. However, Alan also assured me it would be sorted and not to worry. It seemed as though every time we thought we had a plan that would work, another hitch would come along.

The next challenge was deciding how we should sell the tickets and make sure we had an audience. There was no point in recording a DVD for release all over the world if we had no audience. Tina decided the audience should be kept local and she sent letters and posters to every church in the West of Ireland with a contact number. This meant that every Sunday we would know which priest, in what parish, had displayed the poster in the church, as the phone would be hopping with requests for tickets. On Sundays, the sitting room was taken over as we packed envelopes with tickets, ready to post as soon as the cheques arrived, which they always did. Knock Shrine office also sold tickets to anyone who attended the shrine and before we knew it, the concert was heading for a "Sell Out"!

I really wanted the music for the concert to be extra special and in keeping with Monsignor Joe's request that we be respectful of the building. I took an inspirational and spiritual message for the evening and every song chosen had to reflect this theme.

The set also included many of the old songs I was now singing in every concert, like *Hard Times*, *Sand and Water* and *Bright Blue Rose*. All of these fitted in with the overall theme and I couldn't leave them out. After hours of deliberation with the musical director, songs like *Morning Has Broken*, *Bridge Over Troubled Waters*, and *From a Distance* were also introduced. I never thought I would sing songs like those, but suddenly I was finding out more about the type of songs I could sing and I was enjoying every minute of it. My biggest challenge was learning the words of about fifteen new songs, together with all the worry of the set up and running of the show. I would take myself and the dogs off for long walks up the mountains behind my home, listening over and over to the tracks and singing along until I had learned them. I felt a bit old for the 'Cow Shed' and I didn't really want to put my poor Mam and Dad into a spin of wondering why on earth I was back in there, so I hoped the long walks would work.

While these preparations were underway, I was still doing several gigs up and down the country to earn money. Then we decided that in addition to the band, we should have a full orchestra, plus a choir. Special guests were also going to be included, so I asked my old friend Phil Coulter if he would be interested in performing on the show. He duly obliged and once again we were to work together. The other guests were the Donegal singer, Cara Dillon and

Eileen Iver's fiddle player from the USA. This would be my first chance to perform with a full orchestra and now I would experience the real thing for myself. Live! The pressure was really on!

As a break, we took a working trip to South Africa in November. This had been booked earlier in the year and we were looking forward to seeing this amazing country. But when the time arrived, it seemed total madness to be going because of the amount of work still to do at Knock. But we went and the visit to Cape Town was one of the most memorable trips I have ever been on. Not only did we get to visit Robben Island and Table Mountain, but we also got engaged here! It wasn't planned, it just happened on the trip. Our celebrations went on into the night, and during them, Tina hurt her foot. The next morning she had difficulty walking on it. She struggled through that day but the following day the pain was worse. So off we went to the local hospital, only to discover that her leg was broken. Disaster! The only good thing was that we were due to travel home within a couple of days. We had planned to go diving with great white sharks off the coast, but Tina insisted I go with the others from the group and she would stay put in the hotel. To be honest I think she was a little relieved. When we got home I don't know if our families and friends were more shocked that we were engaged or that Tina had a broken leg. Either way, we were straight back into the madness. Between sorting stuff out for the concert and hospital visits for Tina's broken leg, things were manic.

At this point the concert began to catch the imagination of the press and the local radio were covering the buildup. I was in a serious panic about how it would all go. It was now sold out and demand for extra tickets was huge. We had to avoid answering the phone due to the number of requests from people we knew, but there simply were no seats left and we just couldn't fit any more in! We were flat out trying to sort everything, and with Tina on crutches, we had to hire an automatic car to allow her to continue to carry out all her jobs.

It was concert week, early December 2004. The builder arrived a week in advance to build the set and install the sound and light systems. Huge forty foot trucks were arriving daily and unloading their supplies. I went to the Basilica on the second day to review the progress. I nearly died. The place looked like a building site, with lots of people working, building, sawing and hammering. I was terrified that Monsignor Joe would arrive and see what was going on, but as I turned around, there he was, standing beside me. All I could do was apologise for the situation and try and explain that I was in as much shock as he was. But he assured me in his usual calm manner that it was fine and it was a process that had to be gone through to get to the end result! I was relieved that he was okay, but I certainly wasn't. I was still learning my words and going through the show in my head. It suddenly struck me the scale of the disaster that would be upon us if this didn't work!

Two nights before the concert I was scheduled to perform in the famous Waterfront Hall in Belfast. When I'd made this booking, I honestly though it would all fit in fine but when the time came, I saw it was madness to be chasing to Belfast to perform a concert to a huge audience. My good friend Joe Freeley, now a famous taxi man, drove Tina and myself to Belfast. Throughout that journey I felt every emotion possible – fear, apprehension, anxiety and terror! Knock was such a huge undertaking. When we'd set out, we'd had no idea just what a mammoth task we were taking on. But now there was everything to lose. Staging and recording a show of that size costs many hundreds of thousands and it was totally our responsibility.

When we arrived in Belfast, I got into concert mode and focused on the show ahead. Our plan was to travel home immediately after the concert. I got a massive reaction from the Waterfront audience and only when I was relaxed into the show did I realise the importance of where I was playing and how magical the whole concert was. The band with me in Belfast was also going to be in Knock, so it was great to try out some of the songs with them.

Unfortunately during the concert the weather turned horrible, with frost and freezing fog. We couldn't leave Belfast that night so instead we left first thing in the morning. But the fog didn't lift and it took us hours to get to Knock. En route, I got at least thirty phone calls to see where I was. I had completely messed up our carefully prepared schedule and had missed sound checks, camera checks, interviews and rehearsals. Everyone at Knock seemed to be looking for either Tina or me and the tension in the car rose dramatically the nearer we got to the West.

As soon as we pulled up at the Basilica we all jumped out and got straight into dealing with all the problems. Tina was still on crutches and she had to get all the volunteers ready to start work, including every member of our family and all our friends. Four thousand chairs had to be counted and correctly positioned to make sure every one had a view. It was a complete nightmare and it took all night to get the seating right. Then the set ended up being much bigger than planned and we lost several seats on each side. Tina got stuck in organising the whole lot to make sure it was right.

I had to go straight into rehearsals in freezing conditions, as every door was kept open while the crew went in and out fixing sound and lights, as well as building last minute steps and ramps. I worked late into the night on camera checks, lights and sound checks, until I was on the point of exhaustion. Luckily, we had arranged to stay in a hotel in Knock, so in the early hours of the morning that's just what I did.

Right
The concert.

Chapter 50
The Big Night

Left
On stage in the
Basilica in Knock.

We were due to complete more checks and rehearsals the next morning, so imagine my horror when I got up to discover my voice had gone. Yes, it was completely gone! With no voice came no confidence, with no confidence came nervousness and from there I went into emotional turmoil. I was totally terrified. We were at the point of no return with this project and if it didn't take place, we would be ruined! Everything would have to be paid for, regardless of whether the show was staged or not!

I pulled myself together, took honey, lozenges, sat over steam, did a million vocal warm up exercises and went to rehearse. I struggled through the day but I still felt my voice was so bad that it was going to be a disaster. Nobody else seemed at all concerned about my voice but I now realise they were all so busy and stressed trying to get everything else ready, it simply didn't cross their minds that I mightn't be able to perform.

At 4.30pm we were still getting ready when people started to arrive and queue outside. Remember, it was 12th December, absolutely freezing outside and the doors were not due to open until 6.30pm. Everyone worked flat out to get the last things ready and I left to prepare myself in the hotel. What I didn't know at the time was that as soon as I left and they were just about ready to allow the audience into the building, there was a massive power cut. Initially it was thought to be only a temporary cut, but after several phone calls and scrambling around, it was discovered that there was a huge fault which would take some time to repair. Tina had returned to the hotel and was very stressed but was trying to keep me calm, but nobody told me what was happening. I was having a bath when the hotel manager arrived at the room to see if we needed anything. When Tina asked for a cigarette, I knew straight away that something was seriously wrong, because she hadn't smoked for years. I kept asking what the problem was, and all she'd say was that everything was fine.

Tina seemed to be continually on the phone and I couldn't understand what was going on. Only later was I told the full details. The electricity fault would take hours to sort out and there would be no show unless we could get the generators working. My brother-in-law, Smiler, had to climb onto the generators and check if they had enough diesel to get us through the three hours. There were discussions about whether we should postpone the show until the following night but Tina put a stop to that, saying there was no way we could hold everyone over for another night. Plus we had to think of the audience, as many of them had travelled for miles to get there.

At this stage the audience was still outside and the queue now stretched the whole way around the Basilica. People were getting extremely angry. Some of them were losing their patience and taking their anger out on anyone they saw working. Unfortunately it was our families and friends who were getting the worst of it, as they were the volunteers for the night and the abuse they were getting was totally out of control. Once the generators were running, everything had to be rechecked – lights, sound, everything – all the computers had gone down with the power, so they had to be rebooted and checked.

I left for the venue at about 8.00pm, expecting to be on stage within fifteen or twenty minutes, but when I got there, I couldn't understand why people were still queueing outside. It was at this point that Tina informed me that there was a slight delay but nothing to worry about, "It's all sorted now, just focus on what you have to do and just think of that". Of course I didn't do any such thing. I started to panic, thinking we were about to lose the whole show and everything with it, including all our money. And I still didn't know the full extent of the electrical problem.

When I arrived at the Basilica, the musicians and orchestra were all ready and the audience were just starting to come in. But they totally panicked and there was a huge scramble for seats as people lost control and behaved totally inappropriately, considering where they actually were. The only thing that calmed me were the words of Monsignor Joseph Quinn. He said, "Don't worry, when they all settle down, we will leave it in the hands of the Good Lady herself". In fact, it took quite some time for the audience to settle and then we were told by the producer to be on standby.

There was the added problem of not being able to turn on the heating, in case the generators wouldn't be able to keep going for the duration of the concert. Also, with less voltage available, only seventy per cent of the lighting would work. We made the decision to run with the generators, but this meant that even if power was restored, we would have to keep on generator power, as switching over to the mains supply would take too long.

I wanted to go on stage and apologise for what I thought was only a slight delay. I still didn't know how bad things were, but I can understand that everyone thought it best to let me concentrate on my performance. At this point we were still upstairs, waiting for our cue to start. I felt so sick I just wanted to run away.

Then Monsignor Joseph Quinn took to the stage for his introductions and announcements. I heard some of what he said and to this day I'm very proud that he acknowledged me as the creator and gave me credit for the concert, saying "...the idea was the brainchild of one man, Tommy himself". Since then, many others have tried to claim credit for the event, but I can guarantee you not one of them would have stood up and been counted at that moment, with a four thousand-strong angry audience to contend with, a totally confused band, orchestra, choir and guests, plus our families and friends exhausted and abused.

By the time I went on stage I was in such a state I didn't know which of my problems were the biggest. Would my voice hold up? Would the audience fire abuse at me? Would the orchestra, band and choir demand more money for all the confusion and turmoil? I just started to sing and prayed that this might win them over.

And so the concert started. I walked on stage to a cold audience – physically and emotionally. Most of them couldn't understand why they had paid good money for tickets, only to be left queueing outside for so long. I believe I made a stupid remark about the power failure on the stage, which may have only added to the problem. But to be honest, I can't really remember what I said, I was so distraught.

I started to sing one song after the other, mentally chipping away at the set list. All I could see was the end, dear God, please let me get to the end of this concert! I knew Tina was sitting in the audience counting the minutes for more serious reasons – she was praying the generators would keep running, because if the power failed and four thousand people tried to leave the building in complete darkness, then we would really have a problem on our hands.

I noticed that some of the lights at the back of the Basilica weren't working, and it crossed my mind that something must be wrong with them. I had made some mistakes in a few of the songs and these would have to be repeated at the end of the concert. This meant the performing and recording would last over three hours. Little did I know that if I didn't get the timings right to within fifteen minutes, we might well run out of diesel for the generators, and then we'd have some truly serious problems on our hands.

At last the show ended and I was delighted and relieved. Many members of the audience stayed behind to tell me how much they had enjoyed being there and how the music had dispelled any dissatisfaction they'd felt while waiting for the show to begin. I was so happy that people were acknowledging my performance and believe me, it was the hardest performance I had ever delivered in my life!

After the show we went back to the hotel for the post mortem. That was when I learned the full extent of the problems. How on earth had we managed to make this recording! Quite honestly, if it hadn't been for our families and friends, it would never have happened. Now we had to find out if the recording quality was good enough for CD and DVD release. And what about my performance – was it up to standard? I certainly wasn't happy with my voice! We spent the whole night discussing the events of the buildup and I got even more exhausted and headed to bed. Some time later, I was woken by a call from the local radio station. They were looking for a comment on the disaster from the night before. It seemed that some of the audience had contacted the station to make their feelings known.

The radio station had caught the story and was running with it. I agreed to speak on air to explain exactly what had happened and why it had happened the way it did. The interesting thing is that as soon as I did the interview, the calls and complaints stopped and that was it. Some of the local newspapers also picked up the story. They didn't bother to contact me for a comment, they just printed their own version of events. This wasn't very kind or fair, but it was my gig, so I had to take the flack.

For the following few days I had no voice at all. I couldn't speak or sing for at least a week. Tina and I were left exhausted and depressed by the whole experience. It was the most terrifying feeling to know we had worked so hard for so many months, that we had invested everything in it, and now we could be facing a failure. We didn't want to talk about it or discuss it. We just put it out of our minds for a few weeks with the thought, "What have we done and why did we bother?"

Chapter 51
Picking up the pieces

Left
Wrecked!

We didn't do anything with the recordings until the following March. I suppose we didn't want to know the full extent of the disaster that we could be facing. Most of the related running costs were now paid, so we were looking at huge debt. I went back to doing small concerts all over the country to just keep going.

PBS were in contact again and they were looking for the edit and mixing to be finalised and the product made ready for broadcast and sale in August 2005. When we finally did listen and watch the recording, *Voice of Hope*, we were pleasantly surprised and decided to get all the parts in place to release in the USA and Ireland.

Tina and I went to the USA in August for a promotion trip for the release of *Voice of Hope* there. We had seventeen flights in twelve days and took in every imaginable part of the States. This was the less pleasant side of touring. It is very difficult and very exhausting and it brings a whole new level to 'show business' but at least I had something to promote, unlike so many times in the past when these opportunities arose and were missed.

In Ireland, the release was scheduled for 20th October 2005. I had a gig in the Moat Theatre, Naas, on the Friday before the launch date, I was delighted with theatres of this size, as they were working with me to sell the shows and the audiences were amazing. I had a scheduled appearance on The Late Late Show the following week on the night of the release, with the full band and the choir that featured on the DVD. The song chosen was Labi Safris' *Something Inside So Strong*. By sheer coincidence another guest on the show that night was Bishop Desmond Tu Tu, who I'm sure had his own feelings about the song!

We had booked five concerts for November in large thousand seat plus venues to promote the album. Bearing in mind I was coming from smaller venues like Naas that were two hundred seaters, we knew we would have to get some serious promotion going on the back of the appearance on The Late Late Show.

The following morning I had to do a signing and public appearance in Dublin city and during the PA, Tina got one phone call after the other telling us that the concerts were sold out due to the performance on the previous night! These venues included Millennium Forum in Derry, INEC Killarney, and the National Concert Hall, Dublin. All of a sudden we were playing catch up.

By Monday morning we were on the phone booking more venues and second nights in some places. I had to decide what musicians were going to feature and a set list that would feature the new songs, plus the old favorites. At this point I introduced a string quartet to the band, increasing it to a nine piece.

The album reached number three in the charts and sold 100,000 units in its first few weeks. Things were on the up and we were busy, busy, busy, but this time the rewards were ours. Then RTÉ aired the show on national television and it reached another level. The demand for concerts and appearances just spiralled and we were enjoying the relief of a successful project at last.

I was now exactly where I wanted to be, but in the background there was always the issue of the old contracts and these were not going to go away. We knew at some point we were going to have to deal with it all.

Throughout 2005 we worked so hard and things were as good as they could be. We were doing venues like INEC Killarney for three nights, all sold out. I knew I had found what I had been building towards all my working life. Suddenly all the hard work was paying off. We were enjoying it and working on plans for the future, so I suppose you could say I felt liberated! The band had grown, we had permanent crew and a tour manager, we had set up an office with staff, and we had some financial security. Concerts kept selling and the press wanted to talk to me. Things were great.

Chapter 52
Losing my patience!

By 2006, I was still touring and on a creative high, so I decided to put together a new album which I would finance and record myself. I desperately wanted to do a studio album so I went in search of new material. I found what I was looking for after trawling through my collection of songs sent to me, plus my own albums and of course the internet. I decided to approach all the record companies with the new album and I was delighted to get a great offer from Universal Music Ireland. The managing director at the time was Dave Pennyfeather. It was clear from the outset that he and I were going to be able to work together and in fact, this was the beginning of a fantastic relationship. And so *A Life Like Mine* was released. The album was in many ways semi-biographical, as its music and songs reflected exactly where I was in my life at that point. The tracks included *Mystic Lipstick* by Jimmy McCarthy, *Jubilee* from Mary Chapin Carpenter and the old classic, *Four Green Fields*.

We were hoping for a big seller with this release. Okay, so it probably wasn't going to be as special as *Voice of Hope* but with all the new fans now following my music, we believed there was a strong demand for more of my recordings. We made plans for its release. Promotions were set up, advertising was organised, personal appearances arranged and soon everyone was ready to get going, with a huge promotion tour throughout Ireland, North and South. And yes, this time a driver was being provided! I was so proud of this album as it was my first truly independent release, with no ties to anyone. It was due for release on 20th October 2006... the only problem with that was it was the day before our wedding day. Yes, our Wedding Day!

Immediately after *A Life Like Mine* was released, I was sitting at home watching TV, when an advert came on for *A Life Like Mine*. Within a minute or so, another advert appeared for *Voice of Hope* from my previous record company. And then an even bigger surprise which floored me – it was an advert for an album called *The Essential Collection*. What the hell was that? I'd never had an Essential Collection! I knew immediately where it had come from. It seems that while all the pre-release preparations were taking place for *A Life Like Mine*, there was a plan to release an album which included recordings, demos, even songs recorded at concerts that I never knew had been recorded. They were all terrible tracks. In my opinion it was the most unprofessional release I had ever heard on a double album and he released it around the same time as my album.

When the advert for *The Essential Collection* appeared on my TV screen, I just sat stunned, hardly able to believe what I had just seen. I knew my past had caught up with me. It was a disaster! Everyone knew the success *Voice of Hope* had achieved and they all wanted to cash in on a piece of my success.

Below left
On stage in Trafalgar Square, London.

Below right
Left-right Tina. Me, Adam and Linda Burrage.

Chapter 53
My first film appearance

In early January 2006 I received a phone call from an English lady called Linda Burrage, who was living in Glengarriff, County Cork. During the call Linda proceeded to tell me that she had written a poem based on a metal sculpture of a Stag that stands on the cliff overlooking Bantry Bay near her home. The poem is a beautiful and emotional piece of writing that tells the story of all the lonely souls that have been forced to emigrate from Ireland throughout the ages. It relates how many of the emigrants died on the way to their new home or shortly after they arrived. This magnificent Stag, looking out over the bay, symbolizes the calling back of these lost souls to their homeland, to rest in peace.

Linda proceeded to tell me about her wonderful plans to turn this poem into a film and the biggest surprise was that she wanted me to appear in it! Please bear in mind I get calls all the time for weird and wonderful projects, most of which never see the light of day or move past the idea stage. So on my return to bed after talking to Linda for an hour or so, and Tina asked, "Who was on the phone?", my answer was "Some daft dingbat from Cork who has a mad idea about making a film based on a poem she wrote. It will never happen".

Little did I know that I would soon be eating my words, because Linda never let up. She continued to contact me over the next few weeks, asking to meet me as soon as possible. I eventually agreed to meet her in a few week's time, when I was performing in the Cork Opera House, but unfortunately, and much to my embarrassment, I completely forgot all about it and stood her up. This shows how much I believed the film would really happen! Linda and her family approached me after the show and I immediately realised my mistake. I apologised to them and promised that I would meet them a few weeks later in the Glen Eagle hotel in Killarney.

My final show of the tour was in Killarney in late February 2006 and as luck would have it, I was completely exhausted and wiped out with flu, so I spent the day in my hotel room wrapped up in bed. I received a call from reception telling me that the Burrage Family was in reception, waiting to meet me. I could not believe it! I had forgotten yet another meeting! I got myself dressed and went down to meet them.

I arrived into reception to be greeted by Tom, Linda and their daughter Susie. Linda was the most free talking, straight person I had ever met. She didn't stop for a minute, even to take a breath, she talked and talked incessantly about her film and about her vision for it. The more she talked, the more intrigued I became. She read me her two poems, one of which sounded like had been written about me. It later turned out that it was. At that point I was sold on the project. When Linda had finished her sales pitch to me, which I can only put on a par with a heat seeking missile, she asked me what I would charge for my involvement in the film. I replied, "It would be a pleasure to be in your film, let's see how it goes". This woman had won me over completely with her honesty, her vulnerability and most of all her sense of humor.

Throughout the next few months I would make a number of trips to the UK to record songs for the film, one of which was *Through a Childs Eyes*, a song I had recorded for my second album, *Restless Spirit*. The other song, *The Survivors Song*, was written by Linda and Mike Moran. Mike had penned worldwide hits such as *Barcelona* and *Don't Stop Me Now* for Queen and Freddie Mercury. Obviously Linda's charm offensive on Mike had worked even more successfully than on me.

Shooting for the film started in the summer of 2006. Becky, Tina and I headed south to Cork for a couple of weeks, the weather was the warmest it had been in years and we were having a working holiday in County Cork. The first scenes shot were in the local pub, which had been transformed to look like an Irish pub in the middle of New York. It also included about 80 extras in the pub, all dressed from head to toe in Kelly green, with shamrock

Below left
Filming 'The Lonely
Stag'.

Below right
Mike Moran and Me
during filming 'The
Lonely Stag'.

festooned from every hook and knob they could be tied to. I was playing the part of the entertainer in the pub, lip syncing to *The Survivors Song* and dressed in a sparkly Kelly green waistcoat and black shirt. At the end of the song, the Stag could be heard calling the souls back to Ireland. We were then transported back to the 1800s, dressed in heavy woolen trousers and crinoline shirts. The heat was unbelievable and the amount of sweat lost during filming was unimaginable. We then left the pub, transforming into spirits and making our way back to Ireland.

Linda worked as producer, writer and assistant director on the film and boy did she execute her role in all these areas brilliantly. 'The Lonely Stag' film was released a few months later to rave reviews in the USA, where it won several awards, including one at the Myrtle Beach Film festival. A phone call from that "daft dingbat from Cork" in early January, which I had assumed would come to nothing, has instead introduced me to one of my favorite, most admired people and a friend for life. The summer spent making the film was one of my best ever, and it will live with me forever.

Chapter 54
Getting hitched!

Left
Our Wedding Day.

Our wedding was a very special and unique occasion, to say the least. The decision to plan the wedding was only made three weeks ahead of the day itself. It happened while Tina and I were on a visit to Clifden for a concert at the Clifden Arts Festival, enjoying a short break in my favourite hotel, The Ardagh. The plan was hatched while we were relaxing and enjoying ourselves. We knew that with just a few weeks' notice, it was going to be a bit of a scramble to get everything sorted and our families organised, but we decided to keep it to a small, intimate group, just family and close friends. Nothing fussy, but very special.

The date was arranged for Saturday 21st October 2006, and when it came, we were surrounded by everyone we loved, enjoying a weekend-long celebration that was probably quite mad. The look on my parents' faces said it all. They were relaxed and happy, because they knew I was happy and that my career was going well. Dad spent the whole time dancing with anyone who would dance with him, and my Mam looked on pretending to be annoyed, but really very content.

During these happy proceedings, I received a call from Universal Music's solicitor in London. She told me they had received a letter threatening legal action for releasing my new album. If the intention had been to disrupt our wedding, it didn't work. I can honestly say this action didn't in any way upset the happiest day of my life. In fact they had quite the opposite effect. Tina and I continued quite happily with our wedding celebrations and when it came to taking our vows, we didn't just take a vow to each other. We also vowed to sort out this troublesome pest, for once and for all. I was so proud and happy to be marrying the love of my life and I knew we would be a great team in every way from then on.

On Monday morning, immediately after our wedding, I set off on my promotional tour around Ireland, accompanied by my good friend Gerry, who was to be my driver for the next few weeks.

By this stage we were making decent money, so to deal with our case against the ex-manager, we appointed a specialist legal firm with a good reputation for resolving business problems in the entertainment world. Proceedings were issued and the case continued for a few years. We knew we were in for a long, tiresome and expensive roller coaster. But I had handed this over and I had every confidence that it would eventually be resolved, and that I'd have some peace at last.

Left
Left-right Becky, Dad, Tina, Me and Mam on our wedding day.

Chapter 55
The emotional rollercoaster!

We were now facing the biggest challenge of our lives. If we thought Knock had been stressful, it was nothing compared to the trauma of court proceedings. Three separate parties were now fighting for control of my career, and I was hoping to come out of it with my music rights intact and able to continue my career, managed only by Tina and myself. I continued to work and the tours were amazing, as I was now performing with a large band, in the best Irish venues, to full houses. They didn't know it at the time, but everyone who bought a ticket during those years was helping me immensely. Their support meant I was able to continue fighting my legal battles and while I can't thank every fan in person, I'd like to express my gratitude to you all for supporting me at that difficult time. You helped us to get through it.

After several years of legal turmoil, we were drained – emotionally, physically and financially. Anyone who has ever been involved in a legal battle will know the horrible extent to which it impacts on your life and the time it takes to recover from it. And for those of you who haven't had such an experience, I'd advise you to stay well away from it! As it was, I had no choice but to regain my rights, as I knew I couldn't move on in my life and career without dealing with this issue. Otherwise there would always be someone looking for a piece of me and I just couldn't afford to allow this to happen ever again.

I am eternally grateful to Geraldine Clarke and every one at Gleeson McGrath Baldwin for guiding us through it.

Chapter 56
An Antipodean journey

Above left
Tina and Me with her
parents Patsy and Pops
(Padraig) Mitchell.

Above right
(Nanny) Patsy and Me.

Below
On stage during recording
'A Journey Home'.

With all the legal upset going on, I just couldn't settle into a creative mode, so I put together a new show to be recorded in the INEC Killarney. This is how *A Journey Home* was born. It was one of the craziest things I have ever done, as I was still literally fighting for my survival. My idea was to map the journey of Irish music and show how it has travelled around the globe. Seventy million people world-wide claim an Irish heritage. I wanted to reach out to this vast audience with a CD and DVD of Irish songs, old and new, with tunes as diverse as *Raglan Road*, *Danny Boy* and *All I want is You* from U2.

During recording, the experience we had gained from *Voice of Hope* really stood us in good stead, as things went smoothly, with no major crises. Of course, this was a slightly unusual experience for us, because most things we did seemed to result in some sort of drama! *A Journey Home* was released in October 2007. It was a great success and we followed it with a nationwide tour. And there was more good news to follow. As a result of its Irish success, a promoter and record company in Australia showed interest in releasing the album. So Tina and I headed to Australia in June 2008 and met everyone involved in this new project. It was a very exciting time and everything was looking highly positive. The only difficulty was convincing Tina to board a flight to Australia, as she really hates flying, but fair play to her, she plucked up her courage and off we went to explore our new project.

While in Australia, I had meetings with numerous record companies and media promoters, as well as interviews with several radio stations and TV appearances. All of this had to be squeezed into our busy ten-day stay. This hectic schedule meant that each evening, we'd return to our room completely exhausted, but with work still to do. Back in Ireland, our legal team were just beginning their working day. Our legal cases continued, so we would have to spend hours on the phone from Australia, discussing and analysing everything that was going on back home, making offers and contra offers. All the parties involved knew we were in Australia, and although this made decision-making more difficult, we stuck to our guns. No offers were accepted. No conclusions were reached. The matter remained unresolved until we got home.

Finally, in September of 2008, we reached a settlement. We were bruised, battered and financially hurt, but we were finished. I think what I learned most during this awful process was that everything comes to an end. Even things you think will never sort themselves out, always do! I don't wish to go into the exact details of the case but I got everything I wanted – my music, my integrity and my peace of mind.

I was now completely free of anyone connected with my past and I owned all my recordings, everything! At long last it was over. It had been stressful and expensive to gain my freedom but it was the best investment I ever made in my life. I don't just mean my career, but my whole life! I was now free to do whatever I wanted, to sing what I wanted, to record what I wanted, without being involved with people who just didn't care. It was over!

To add to all the legal stress, we had a much bigger problem to deal with. Tina's Mum, Patsy, had been unwell early in 2008 and after a series of tests and investigations, she was diagnosed with cancer in March of that year. This was a massive blow that we hadn't seen coming. Her diagnosis was quickly followed by treatments involving hospital visits and stays. Time moved very quickly and we all thought she would pull through. Patsy was a born fighter and one of the healthiest people I have ever known, someone who looked after herself well, with regular exercise, a healthy diet and all the things that the rest of us should do, but usually don't.

We spent month after month finding out about her disease and investigating various treatments, but to our total shock and dismay, we lost Patsy on 17th December 2008. It was one of the most traumatic experiences we had ever gone through. It was hard enough having to deal with her loss, but trying to accept how she had suffered and fought for life during her illness left its own deep scars too. We had never experienced anything so profoundly painful before and were trying to understand 'Why?' We all missed Patsy terribly and found it very hard to adjust to life without her. I know how much her loss hurt me, so I can't imagine how Tina and the kids felt. We tried to help each other as much as we could, but grieving is a painful process that only time can heal.

Chapter 57
The best is yet to come!

After the court settlement, Tina and I were at last in control of our own ship. We were now able to make decisions to suit ourselves and work suddenly became a joy. It had all been worthwhile. To celebrate our legal closure, I decided to release a new album featuring my favourite recordings. This would be an official 'best of' double album – one that would radically outclass *The Essential Collection*.

I called the album *The Best is Yet to Come*. The name reflected where I felt I was in my career – this was a new start and that the best of my recordings and concerts were yet to come. With my new-found creative freedom, I was able to really enjoy this release and its follow up tour. I had complete peace of mind, knowing that no-one was going to appear out of the blue and cause problems.

The album was a complete success and gave us the impetus to get touring outside Ireland, so we planned a full nationwide tour of Australia. During April and May of 2009, I toured throughout this fabulous country. It was all so exciting! I was in complete control and I felt like a teenager again. The promoter had done a first-class job before we arrived and audience bookings were healthy. I was so looking forward to this tour!

I arrived a week ahead of the band in order to complete some pre-tour promo work, then we opened our first night in Melbourne with a fantastic crowd and a great show. Afterwards, I was tired, so I headed to bed, only to wake the next morning with terrible tonsillitis. I took antibiotics and pain relief but they didn't work and I went through the next three weeks of the tour with a severe throat infection.

Despite this, I struggled on through every concert and wouldn't allow any of them to be cancelled. Every night it was the same routine. I'd go to bed immediately after the show, hoping to wake up fully recovered the next morning. But no! I just had to struggle on, feeling more and more sorry for myself every day.

The more ill I became, the more I found myself missing Tina and home. I honestly found it difficult to keep going, but somehow I did.

This wasn't the way it was supposed to be. This was my big tour and I was supposed to be enjoying the experience, but I just couldn't shake off the infection. I actually didn't fully recover until I had been home for quite a while. But despite all of this, my Australian tour had been deeply rewarding and my illness certainly didn't put me off going back again.

Left
Recording the album 'Going Back' with Paul McAteer my drummer, Joe Csibi my double bass player, Ewan Cowley my guitar player, and Conal Early, guitar with David Hayes on piano.

Right
Outside Sydney Opera House, Australia.

Chapter 58
Happy Christmas!

Left
Ewan, Me and Conal
performing in Knock
Basilica 2009.

Below left
Left-right Michelle Mason,
Me, David and Conal
recording 'Song For A
Winter's Night' – Belleek
Castle, Ballina.

Once my throat had recovered and I got well rested (and stopped feeling sorry for myself), I started to get itchy feet again and wondered what I should do next. One of my problems (or maybe it's a strength) is that I can't sit still for long once I've finished a project. So as soon as I had rested up after Australia, I needed something else to focus on. And that's when I got the idea of recording a Christmas Album for release later in the year.

I wanted to record some of the special Christmas songs I learned as a child – songs that were special to my parents and to me. So I spent the only good week of weather in July of that year, locked in the recording studio with David, recording wonderful tracks like *O Holy Night*, *Walking in the Air* and *Christmas 1915*. It was certainly a bizarre experience to be singing Christmas songs in the height of summer!

I decided to support the release of the Christmas album by recording a DVD set in Belleek Castle, Ballina. It was planned to be released at the same time as the album. Although it was a much smaller production than either of my two previous DVDs, it had a beautiful castle setting and I was accompanied by my band. It includes many Christmas tracks and several other acoustic-type tracks. The Christmas album was called *Song For A Winter's Night*. It is a very special recording to me. I feel it captures the magic of Christmas time, something we experience every year from our childhood.

For the release of *Song For A Winter's Night*, I was offered another chance to perform on The Late Late Show. This time I would be singing one of my all time favourite songs, *Christmas 1915*. The line up for the show included Michael Bublé, who of course is a huge international star, so I felt a little insecure in his presence. Then something rather strange and wonderful happened. I was back stage, warming my voice before my performance, when Michael approached me and asked how I had managed to hit the note I had just sung, as he couldn't reach it! I was absolutely chuffed to bits at his compliment. I never ask for photographs or autographs from the famous people I meet, but this is one occasion when I regret not getting a memento!

Christmas 1915 is a beautiful and tragic song. It tells the story of a young man fighting at the front in the First World War. On Christmas Day, 1915, the Allies and Germans call a truce, lay down their arms and share what little they have until the following day, when they go back to the horror of war. This song has remained in my set list ever since its release and I perform it all year around. The amount of people who request it time and time again is phenomenal. *Song For A Winter's Night* continues to sell well and even I love listening to it, something I rarely do with my own albums!

I got another crazy idea during the late summer of 2009. I decided to stage another concert at the Basilica in Knock. No recordings, just a concert to be performed by me and enjoyed by the audience. And this time there would be no sitting around in freezing conditions with endless hours of interruptions and recordings. The fifth anniversary of the original concert was approaching and I wanted to prove that the Basilica could be a very special place for a very special event. I also wanted to show everyone who had suffered through the first concert with me that it hadn't all been in vain.

We were granted permission to use the venue and we set about organising and selling the event. Mind you, the experience we had acquired over the last few years meant it was all much easier this time around. We were much more organised and we used properly trained, professional people to help run every aspect of the concert.

The concert took place on 12th December 2009 and it was unforgettable. For me, it was both a pleasure and a privilege to perform in such a special place, in front of such a receptive audience, and with no intrusions from cameras and crew. It was an amazing experience to be able to deliver one exquisite song after another to the audience. At the end of the concert, I felt a huge sense of achievement and release. It was as if I could finally let the ghost of 2004 rest in peace, and move on.

Christmas 2009 was soon upon us. It was the winter of the deep freeze, when we had sub-zero temperatures for days on end, and lows of minus 20 degrees centigrade on several nights. It was a strange Christmas, our first without Patsy and with the weather so bad, we were mostly housebound. Many roads were completely impassable and it was very difficult to visit Mam and Dad, as their house was half way up the mountain. For the first time in my life, I had the sense of what it was like to be without a parent and it made the reality of my own parents' mortality very real.

After the thaw, and New Year, it was back to normal, with more touring and more concerts, but without any stresses and strains. In fact, working like this had become very much the norm for me, to the extent that I had almost forgotten what it had been like in the past, when I was continually stressed out. Work was now calm and normal, and life continued without any outside interference. It was great.

Chapter 59
Looking back

Left
Peter Kenny of Indi
Entertainment, Me
being presented with a
Platinum Disc for sales of
'Going Back', alongside
Sinead O'Connor, RTÉ
Commercial Enterprises.

As time passed, and I began to realise that life wouldn't last forever, I found myself being more and more influenced by the musical tastes of my parents. Dad had always loved big singers and big orchestral sounds, and thinking about this musical genre got me into creative mode once again. So, I started planning to record a number of big ballads and classic numbers using a full orchestra. What's more, I decided to dedicate it to my parents. I knew Dad's love of these songs would make the recording very special to him. Mam was easier to please she always loved anything I did!

All the research for this album would be done in my parent's house, sifting through the vast musical library I'd listened to throughout my childhood. I was going to include songs that I always wanted to record but had shied away from, for fear they were too big for me. This turned out to be one of the most enjoyable and innovative recording experiences of my career, and it was fantastic to sing with a full orchestra. The subsequent CD and DVD releases, titled *Going Back*, included such classics as *Softly As I Leave You*, *You'll Never Walk Alone* and a most unusual choice, *Tell Me It's Not True*, from Blood Brothers.

All the songs on *Going Back* mean a great deal to me. They bring me back to a place where I feel safe and warm, a place where I belong. They remind me of lazy Sundays lying on the couch in our sitting room, with Dad playing his favourite songs on the record player and Mam completing her 'Spot the Ball' entry. She did this every Sunday without fail, and sent it off with the £1 entry fee. Spot the Ball was a newspaper competition which featured a picture of a football match, with the ball removed. You had to mark X where you thought the ball was. Well, after years of trying and numerous £1 entries, Mam finally won the £2000 prize. Of course, she was delighted, telling us that it really had paid to be entering every week for all those years! Memories like these inspired me to record *Going Back*. Today they form a memory bank that's so special, I sometimes rely on it to get me through tough times.

A documentary-style DVD for *Going Back* was due to be filmed at RTÉ in August, but was brought forward to June. This threw everything into chaos. I had songs to rehearse, charts to write and everything had to be completed within a few days. Eventually the recording day arrived and I walked into RTÉ to perform with the RTÉ Concert Orchestra. It was an unbelievable experience – one I never expected to happen. As soon as I walked into the studio and heard the arrangements for those wonderful songs being played, I was transported back to that amazing place in my childhood.

We recorded all day as we needed thirteen songs for the DVD. The problem was that each song had to be performed over and over, so I probably sang around 40 tracks that day, just to get the thirteen songs for the DVD. I spent the entire day standing in the middle of the orchestra, singing my heart out. Towards evening time, I was struggling to keep going. My legs and back were aching and my voice was having difficulty reaching the big notes.

After the recording, Tina and I headed straight home to Sligo and I went to bed, completely exhausted. The following morning I knew something was not quite right, as I couldn't walk without severe pain. I thought it was probably due to the long hours I'd been standing the day before. But I was wrong. I had actually ruptured discs in my back and I had to go into hospital for immediate surgery. All I could think of was, "Oh no, not again". Once more, an injury was throwing me into emotional turmoil. How would this affect me. How long would I be out of action? Would it impact on my mobility? Everything I'd planned for the new album would be on hold!

Some of the tracks had already been recorded, so I had to hand the project over to David Hayes and let him finish it without me. My focus had to be on getting better. I was lucky because I had a brilliant surgeon and the operation went smoothly, and this time I decided to allow the professionals to do their job and follow their advice. I didn't want to lose any more precious time getting well.

I was released from hospital in Dublin four days after the surgery. I knew the Irish Concert Orchestra was recording some of the tracks in Windmill Lane studios, so I hatched a cunning plan. Once Tina had picked me up, and I was safely propped up in the car, surrounded by pillows for the journey home, I managed to convince her to drive past the studio... just to see what was going on. Big mistake! I hadn't realised I'd have to climb three flights of stairs to reach the recording studio. Getting up those stairs was crazy, but I did it. Getting down them again was a bit more tricky!

The orchestra was in full flow when I arrived, with David frantically conducting away, trying to get the best out of each and every musician. My emotions got the better of me, I just couldn't believe the magical sound that was all around me. I was already in an emotionally fragile state and listening to this music only heightened my condition. I just wanted to stay there and get stuck right into the middle of it but I knew I wasn't well enough. Eventually I gave in and we headed for home, where all I wanted to do was curl up and cry.

I felt quite upset on the journey home, probably because of a combination of factors – drugs for my injury, thoughts of what I was missing and of course, a lot of self pity. The following few weeks were pretty rough and I was fit for nothing but bed. But I found that lying there brought back too many memories of my car accident, so as soon as I was able, I made myself get up and get on with things. Within a couple of weeks I was back recording, and after three weeks, I was heading for the Cleveland Irish Music Festival and then on to a week-long promotion trip to Australia. It was tough. The scars on my back was still very fresh, as were the scars in my psyche from 1998.

That was one crazy summer, with new recording experiences, serious illness and international travel to deal with. Little wonder I was exhausted by the end of it. The album was finished and plans were in place for its release, but before that, Tina and I went on a week's holiday together. Immediately afterwards, I headed off for my second tour of Australia. Another

flight and more time away from home, and while I enjoyed the tour very much, I was constantly preoccupied with thoughts of home and the length of time I was going to be away.

I found myself wishing the time away, conscious of the fact that I was so far from home and anxious in case anything would happen while I was away. I felt really helpless and to make matters even worse, I got another bout of tonsillitis. I now know that every time I travel, I'm likely to get this, so I have to prepare myself and be on my guard to avoid it.

I was happy to get back home after the tour. *Going Back* was released and I enjoyed every minute of the promotion work and touring for that album. We decided to tour Ireland with a full orchestra, so I put together a show with my own band and the Irish Concert Orchestra and we had a hugely successful tour all over Ireland. I loved that experience. It also meant that the audience who had been with me all through the years, and who had seen me start my career with two musicians, then five and then nine, were now watching me perform with a full orchestra.

Below left
During one of the concerts with Irish Concert Orchestra.

Below right
My pleasure to meet Mícheál Ó Muircheartaigh - the 'voice of Gaelic games'.

Chapter 60
My collection, the official one!

In the summer of 2011, after an exhausting few months of touring, Tina and I started to clear out some old office files and rubbish that had gathered up over the years. I came across some old demo tapes on an old digital master tape (DAT) of one of my first ever recordings, *Loving Hannah*, recorded in 1991. Curiosity got the better of me and I had to have a listen. I couldn't believe how clear and fresh it sounded. After a couple of listens, Tina reminded me that it was twenty years old and she suggested that I should do something to celebrate those two decades and commemorate this milestone. At first I was reluctant, but as the days passed and I gave it more thought, it started to make some sense. The big question was, what to do?

We decided to produce an album that would reflect my career over the past twenty years. The next problem, where to begin with the material. Was it going to be a double album? Should there be a DVD? What was I going to do?

Eventually we decided on a double album, so I set about choosing the thirty songs that best reflected my twenty-year career, from the highs and the lows, to the absolute sublime. It was a mammoth task, compiling a list of songs, then choosing some and discarding others. It often seemed like one step forward, three steps back. Far too many people were telling me what they wanted to hear on the album, and it wasn't helping me at all. I listened to every live recording we had ever made, from the Recital Hall in Sydney, to the Concert Hall in Dublin. I knew there would be magical moments captured on some of the live recordings that I wouldn't find on studio recordings such as *The Rose* and *The Orchard*. There were also duets that I was extremely proud of and wanted them to make the cut. So much choice, so little time!

We ended up with far too many songs for a double album, so it became a triple CD collection. Disc one, the Irish Collection, disc two, The Contempory Collection, and Disc three, The Duets Collection. In all, 40 songs, 20 years, three CDs and an album titled *The Platinum Collection*. I guess it was a sort of anthology, which is probably a little ambitious when you are only 41, but let's call it that anyway!

The album was released in the autum, and it reached number four in the album charts, becoming one of the best selling 'Best of' collections to date. When I look back on all the work and the hours that Tina and I put into *The Platinum Collection*, I have to admit it's the one project of which I am most proud. I remind myself that it was created with the help of amazing people who contributed massively to my career.

The album has since been released in several countries, with tours and public appearances following every release. Which of course has meant more flights, more radio and TV stations, press, photos and all the work that goes with releasing a new album! Interestingly though, the release of *The Platinum Collection* produced a shift in how the press viewed both the album, and me. For some reason they seemed to think it was my swan-song album – that I was finally hanging up my musical boots and taking early retirement. Of course, that was completely ludicrous, as I'm only 41, and there's lots of music still left in me. But no matter how much I protested and talked about my other projects, they still reported that I was going to retire. I wish!

I started to tour the album again in late 2011, but this time the touring was tinged with doubt and guilt. My Dad had been unwell for a number of months and although his illness seemed to have come out of nowhere, if I'm honest I had noticed some changes in his health over the previous year. I suppose I just didn't want face the fact that life was moving on. By November 2011, his health was fading and I found it hard to deal with. I can handle the physical side of illness but I find mental deterioration and emotional disturbances much more difficult to accept.

I suppose I'll always feel anger towards part of my Dad's illness. It will take many years to accept it and perhaps I never will. As the weeks and months passed, and with every visit home, the changes in Dad were becoming ever more apparent. Most days he knew who I was and what I did. However there were times when he didn't, and those times chipped away at me and they still hurt to this day. Here was my Dad, the man I knew and loved all my life, the man I knew could protect me when I was growing up, and now he was becoming dependent on his children for his care. How ironic and frightening!

I found it extremely difficult to carry on a normal life and career. Whatever my feelings may have been, Dad's condition took a much bigger toll on my Mam. She was the one who always worried about the slightest thing and who sat by his side for fifty-plus years. I'm sure she must have found it very sad during these times.

In Early December Dad was admitted to hospital for observation, tests and a general check on his health. Every time I visited him I saw a change, although other family members say they didn't notice anything. Perhaps I was really looking for a positive change... something to show an improvement since my last visit, but it was never to be. After a few days in hospital, Dad was discharged and sent home. This was a huge relief for Mam and all of us, as we had a feeling this could be the last Christmas we would spend with him!

Chapter 61
Our final Christmas

Left
Mam and Dad.

Christmas 2011 arrived with its usual fuss and mayhem. The kids were much older and wiser, so for a few years, Santa has not been the priority. Socialising was much more important.

I spent as much time as I possibly could with Mam and Dad. Mam and I talked at length so I knew she was becoming increasingly concerned about Dad. As I write this, I firmly believe that music was the best career I could have chosen, whenever Dad didn't know me in person, he would always recognise my singing. So we constantly played my DVDs and CDs to him and he would sit quite happily for hours listening to them, aware that it was me. I believe that somewhere in his world, he was still very proud of me and I will always be grateful for those moments of clarity.

With Christmas and New Year behind me, I went back to work in late January 2012. I was very glad to be touring Ireland, as this meant I could be near home at all times. Of course, there were the usual worries about whether the concerts would sell and how our new songs would go down. But that was the usual stuff that goes with touring and we needn't have worried. Our loyal Irish audiences came out in force to see us, for which we are always very grateful! The audience reactions were brilliant and the shows got very positive reviews. But there was a sadness in me that I couldn't explain. Some might say it was depression, but I believe that's a word that's over-used, especially by people in the public eye. I wasn't depressed. I was just sad and guilty and I felt completely selfish when it came to my Mam and Dad. Yes, reality was staring me in the face. They were getting older and to use one of Mam's favourite sayings, "Time and tide wait for no man". I was approaching my own middle age and was coming to see that Mam and Dad were no longer as fit and healthy as they had once been. This upset me greatly and I found it hard to accept.

In the early part of 2012, my sister Marie started planning a family get together to celebrate Mam and Dad's 50th Wedding Anniversary. They had married each other on the 5th March, 1962 and for the next 50 years, did everything together. They even had their rows in an organised way! I never imagined I would find myself admiring their marriage and aspiring to model it. But nor were they angels and I am sure they had healthy disagreements about things, just like every other couple. The point is they definitely shared something very special, although we didn't realise it while we were growing up.

On the 3rd March 2012 we were all at home celebrating Mam and Dad's 50th anniversary and honouring this milestone event. When Tina and I arrived, the house was full and I couldn't help but notice how much the dynamics of the family had changed. There used to be only just six siblings and Mam and Dad in this big farmhouse but now, with spouses and grandchildren, it had increased to twenty four! Mam and Dad always beamed with pride to see us all together and the look of contentment on their faces told us they were proud to see us happy and successful in our own fields.

The celebration started with mass in the house. Mam's faith always played a huge part in her life, so this was compulsory. I honestly believe her faith helped get us through any crises that arose in our lives. During the mass, Mam and Dad renewed their marriage vows, this was a very moving and poignant moment for me. It is a profound experience to witness your parents renewing their wedding vows, fifty years after they first said the words "I do"!

Once the formal part was over, we all tucked into the family meal. This had been prepared by all my sisters and my Brother JJ, who certainly cooks a mean ham! And just to make sure we all knew, he reminded us of it several times during our feast. It was a day was full of stories and memories of our childhood and adolescent years – some very funny, others less so. I found it to be a strange day, but in a good way, because it brought home my own mortality and how time can pass by in a flash. I had always found our family gatherings to be very happy occasions but when the time came to go home, I experienced a feeling of sadness, perhaps because another milestone had passed and none of us knew what lay ahead.

I had a few days off from performing and in the days following the anniversary celebrations, Tina and the crew were busy organising the UK tour and the final date of the Irish tour, due to be on 8th March in The Grand Canal Theatre, Dublin. This was the most exciting night of all the performances I ever had in Dublin. It is a special place, with a capacity of over 2000. However there were a few complications. Conal, my main guitar player, had lost his Uncle a day or so before the show and was unable to play. He had been very close to his uncle and his grief was heartbreaking. We had a nervous time trying to replace him for the show and despite David's constant reassurances that everything would be fine, I was not so sure. I had been building up to this show for months and any glitches at this point would totally throw me and put my performance under pressure.

Tina and I left Sligo for Dublin early on Thursday morning, as I needed to be there in good time to rehearse with the new guitar player, Jack Maher. I get pretty blindsided when there's a major change in the line up of the band, especially at such short notice. I was worried because we hadn't heard from Conal for a few days, despite leaving him some messages. Then just as we were driving into Dublin, he called me. He was doing okay and wondered if I still needed him that night, he said he would be able to play for the show. My face lit up! This must be what it's like to win the lottery! It was the best gift anyone could have given me. I now knew the show would be okay and the bonus was I now had two guitarists, only a few days before I'd had none! Typical! I was happy that our last night in Ireland would be a huge success.

At four minutes past 8.00pm, I walked onto the stage to the biggest welcome I'd ever received in all my twenty years. From the first word I sang that night, everything moved with ease like a well oiled machine. There were a number of times when I looked over at Conal to see how he was holding up and I knew he was breaking from the inside out. But the only thing we could do was let him know we were there for him. The show lasted over two hours and after the final song I couldn't contain my emotions – I cried with happiness at the audience's reaction. It was the best show of my life and will probably remain so for a very long time.

I went with some friends and band members to the after party where someone pointed out that I had mentioned my parents a lot on stage and that I'd told family stories that related to the songs I was singing. I hadn't previously been aware of this and thought nothing of it at that time.

Left
Performing with Irish
Concert Orchestra.

Chapter 62
Where to begin?

The following morning I flew to Manchester to start publicity for the ten-date UK tour, then it would be straight into the tour itself. This was my second UK tour as a solo artist and my first with the entire band and crew. I took an early morning flight to Manchester, I had been invited to officially open the Manchester Irish festival in Manchester town hall. After arriving at my hotel I grabbed a few hours rest and then made my way to the town hall, where I launched the festival and performed at the opening ceremony. I met with the festival organisers and officials, then slipped back to my hotel to get some rest, before a three-hour train ride from Manchester and the first UK show in Bristol the following day.

I boarded the train at around 10.30am on Saturday, 10th March with great expectations for the day and night ahead. We had put months of work into the tour and I had travelled all over the UK on several promotion trips in the months leading up to it. Finally it was here. A new territory and a new audience. This was exciting!

I love to travel by train in the UK as almost all of them have first-class cabins, where you can sit back and relax for the few hours it takes to reach your destination. The train was just coming into Bristol when my phone rang. It was Tina and I knew immediately from her tone of voice that something was wrong. She proceeded to calmly explain that Mam had suffered a stroke, but not to panic as she would be okay!

Mam had suffered from a stroke on her left side eight years previously and had made a full recovery. So when Tina told me that this time it was her right side, my heart sank! Deep down I knew there would be no happy ending!

Throughout that day my sister Cathy and Tina filled me in on that was happening. They tried to reassure me that everything was okay and that Mam was being well looked after. From that day onwards, I carried a feeling of loneliness and isolation, perhaps because I was away from home and feeling completely and utterly helpless. I desperately wanted to go back home but there was no sense doing so unless Mam's condition deteriorated dramatically, or until the prognosis had been established. I pulled myself together to get on stage and perform the concert, but I can honestly say it was one of the hardest things I've ever had to do. I performed two more shows until we arrived at the O2 Shepherd Bush Empire for the London show.

While I was resting in the dressing room, Cathy called me to say that Mam's condition was deteriorating and that I should get home as fast as I could. Tina had now joined me in the UK and we frantically checked and booked flights in and out of Ireland over the next few days, to cover all eventualities. It was too late to get out of London that night, and showtime was already upon us with a full house of new fans, so we decided to go ahead with the concert rather than cancel. Instead, the plan was that after the show I would go with my brother-in-law Brendan, who lived in London, he would drive me to the airport early in the morning and I could fly back home. I had never felt so profoundly sad in all my life! I can only apologise to the audience who were there, as I have no idea how I managed to stand in front of them and I certainly didn't give them the performance they deserved.

I arrived back in Ireland the next morning. My brother-in-law, Mort, collected me from the airport and drove me to the hospital where my Mam was being cared for. I spent a couple of days with Mam, visiting her in the hospital. Her condition was stable but critical. Eventually, after speaking with my brothers, sisters and the medical staff, I decided to return to Glasgow and continue the UK tour. If I'd had a choice I would have cancelled the entire tour, but the contractual arrangements meant I had to try and fulfil my obligations. I hated every minute I was in the UK. After the Glasgow show, there was Birmingham and then on to Cardiff, where I got another phone call from Cathy with more bad news. She told me that Dad had now been admitted to hospital with heart failure and that I should return home straight away. At this point we had to make some realistic decisions, so I cancelled all the remaining shows. I honestly hadn't the head space to deal with work and I didn't care what the consequences of this would be. I just wanted to get home to see my Mam and Dad.

Conal drove me to the airport and I flew into Dublin where my friend Gerry collected me and drove me to meet Tina. A few hours later, in the early hours of the morning, we arrived at the hospital in Castlebar. I went to Mam's bed to find her sleeping comfortably. Dad was also very comfortable at this point. I was overwhelmed with sadness, not knowing what to do to try and make this situation better. I knew that they were both seriously ill, so I had to try and pull myself together to deal with this.

My Mam had not spoken a word since she had been admitted the previous week. I found her inability to speak very difficult to deal with. I just wanted her to let me know she was okay, but I got my chance to speak to her over the coming days. We knew by this stage that Mam would not be getting any better, nor would she be coming home with us, but things were not quite as serious with Dad. We hoped he would recover enough to deal with Mam's stroke and return home.

Over the coming days, I spent every moment I could with them, secretly hoping and praying that everything would turn out alright... and wishing this might come true for all of us!

On the 30th March, at 9.15am, our beloved Mam passed away very peacefully. We were all with her and were relieved that her suffering over the last ten days was over. But we were numb with grief! I didn't know it was physically possible to have such an ache in your heart, but it is! My heart bled for the loss of our dear Mam. It's a pain I'll never be able to describe. Shortly after she passed away we had to tell Dad. He was in the ward across the corridor from her, and he wept when he was told the news. It broke our hearts to see him in this state and we wondered how he would cope without her!

The staff of Mayo General Hospital showed a wonderful level of care and compassion to my parents while they were there. We were also treated with great kindness as we went through the turmoil of what was happening. A few hours after Mam left us, we set about making arrangements for her funeral. We decided that she should be brought home that evening and waked overnight, then taken to the funeral home the following evening and buried on Sunday.

That night, after a visit home for a shower and clothes, we all returned to the hospital to accompany Mam back to our family home. Our first task was to visit Dad and see if he was okay. The nurses assured us he was sleeping quite comfortably and that we should go and do what we had to do. They would be in touch if there was any change. We all travelled the road home with Mam and laid her out in the sitting room. Her arrival at the house was one of the most upsetting things I have ever gone through. Just watching the grandchildren welcome Nanny home in a coffin was incredibly moving and upsetting for us all. Neighbours and relatives joined us in the following hours and it was the first time for days that all six of us had been together outside the hospital. When things settled and we'd had a bite to eat, we called the hospital to see how Dad was doing. We were told, "He's comfortable". At that point we discussed who should return to the hospital, as we were worried about leaving Dad alone on this awful night.

At 11.30pm, the house phone rang. My brother Patrick answered it and no one really paid him much heed, as the phone had been ringing all evening. When he hung up we took one look at him and he uttered the dreadful words, "Dad's died". Our world was thrown into complete turmoil. Our wonderful, loving Dad had also passed away. None of us could comprehend what was happening! It must be a mistake! In that moment, our lives were turned upside down. We had now lost the two most precious people in our lives, our Mam and Dad.

We went through exactly the same routine the following day and decided to hold back Mam's funeral for a day to allow them to have the same ceremony. Dad was brought home and a feeling of numbness still afflicted us. We simply could not believe what had happened. The weekend was filled with a constant flow of people paying their respects and conveying their disbelief at the loss of Mam and Dad in the one day.

If I am honest, I found some comfort in the knowledge that they were now together, as they had been for the previous fifty years. It was the only comfort I could find during what I can only ever describe as the worst period in my life. I had lost friends and relatives over the years and had grieved for them, but this grief was totally different. It is a wound that will take years to heal.

Mam and Dad's funeral took place in the local church in the village of Kilmactigue where they were married, where I grew up and where they raised all six of us for most of our lives. I sang at the funeral, which was one of the most difficult thing I have ever done in my life, but I'm so glad now that I sang for them both, one more time. I take some comfort from my belief that they are still watching out for us all from their sanctuary.

In the months that followed I experienced every emotion humanly possible. There's not a day goes by that I don't speak to Mam and Dad in some form, be it a prayer or just quietly telling them that I'm ok! I have performed a few shows since Mam and Dad passed but I still haven't mustered up the strength to undertake a full international tour, although that will come in time. Everyone tells me time is a great healer, but in this instance, I wish time would move a little faster!

I'm now in the lonely position of feeling my own way in life without having my parents to bounce ideas off, or having the security of going home and just knowing they are there. I suppose I was blessed to have had them in my life for forty one years but I still feel cheated, and I think I am way too young to have lost them both.

There are so many more stories and tales I could tell you, but of all the stories and tales I have chosen, the most important ones are those that are relevant to my life and my music. Someday I will recount those stories, but not yet! Now I must start a new chapter of my life without my beloved parents here with me, but they live on in my memories and I know are looking down on me with their guiding love!

Now! Let me Begin!

Leabharlanna Poibli Chathair Bhaile Átha Cliath
Dublin City Public Libraries

Dedicated in loving memory
to my Mam and Dad